Gardening in Containers

Created and designed by the editorial staff of ORTHO BOOKS

Project editor
Ken Burke

Editor
Alvin Horton

Designers
Craig Bergquist
Christine Dunham

Illustrator
Ron Hildebrand

Ortho Books

Publisher
Robert L. Iacopi

Editorial Director
Min S. Yee

Managing Editor
Anne Coolman

Horticultural Editor
Michael D. Smith

Senior Editors
Kenneth R. Burke
Sally W. Smith

Production Manager
Laurie Sheldon

Horticulturists
Michael D. McKinley
Deni W. Stein

Production Assistant
Darcie S. Furlan

Editorial Assistants
Laurie A. Black
Anne D. Pederson
William F. Yusavage

National Sales Manager
Garry P. Wellman

Operations/Distribution
William T. Pletcher

Operations Assistant
Donna M. White

Administrative Assistant
Georgiann Wright

Address all inquiries to:
Ortho Books
Chevron Chemical Company
Consumer Products Division
575 Market Street
San Francisco, CA 94105

First Printing in August, 1983

1 2 3 4 5 6 7 8 9
83 84 85 86 87 88

ISBN 0-89721-020-4

Library of Congress Catalog Card
Number 83-61314

Chevron Chemical Company
575 Market Street, San Francisco, CA 94105

Acknowledgments
Typography by
Typothetae
Palo Alto, CA

Color separations by:
Color Tech
Redwood City, CA

Additional illustration by:
Ronda Hildebrand
David Hildebrand

Research assistance by:
Dodge Ely

**Copy editing and Production
editing by:**
Jessie Wood
editcetera
Berkeley, CA

Proofreading and indexing by:
editcetera
Berkeley, CA

Photography:
(Names of photographers in
alphabetical order are followed
by page numbers on which their
work appears. R = right,
C = center, L = left, T = top,
B = bottom.)

William Aplin: 74TL, 75TL, 75BL

Martha Baker: 20B, 23T, 24CL,
35TL, 75BR

Laurie A. Black: 4, 7BL, 23, 24T,
25T, 40B, 44T, 48, 57R, 66R,
72, 74BR, 77T, 77B, 78L, 79TL,
79BL, 80, 91T

Clyde Childress: 40T, 55R

Josephine Coatsworth: 24CR,
37R, 38L, 51BR

Derek Fell: 20TL, 30L, 32R, 34L,
47R, 52L, 61, 74TR

Pamela Harper: 36L

Susan Lammers: 60

Michael Landis: 7T, 9, 20TR,
36R, 38R, 50, 62L, 65T,
65B, 66BL

Michael McKinley: 5, 20C, 21,
26, 34TR, 34BR, 35R, 42B,
55TL, 58, 63L, 66TL, 67L, 68L,
68R, 79TR, 84, 86, 87L, 87R,
88, 89T, 89C, 89B, 90T, 90B,
91B, 93T, 93C, 93B

James McNair: 6BL, 6BR, 7BR,
43L, 43R

Jack Napton: 49, 75TR

Ortho Books: 6TL, 6TR, 8,
14BL, 14BR, 18, 19, 24B, 25C,
25B, 28L, 28R, 29L, 29R, 30R,
31L, 32L, 32C, 33L, 33R, 35BL,
37L, 37C, 39L, 39R, 42TL,
42TR, 44B, 45L, 51L, 51TR,
52, 53, 54, 55BL, 57L, 62R,
63R, 69L, 69R, 83L, 83R,
92T, 92B

Michael D. Smith: 38C, 56

George Taloumis: 31R, 45TR,
45BR, 47L

Tom Tracy: 67R, 71TL,
71TR, 71BR

Wolf von dem Busche: 82

Special thanks:
Pamela Pierce
San Francisco, CA

Carol and Bill Uber
Van Ness Water Gardens
Upland, CA

Joe Sakuma
Bonsai grower and technical
services
Palo Alto, CA

Front cover: Fred Lyon. Long-lasting color in containers is provided by pink and white impatiens and pink geraniums. The rhododendrons in the background have just finished blooming.

Back cover: *Top left:* Fred Lyon. Clockwise from bottom left, container plants include echeveria, pink and white impatiens, hydrangeas, rhododendrons, cymbidium, jade plant, ageratum, iberis, and kalanchoe. *Top right:* Josephine Coatsworth. *Thunbergia alata. Bottom left:* Derek Fell. Fuchsia 'Jack Shahan'. *Bottom right:* Clyde Childress. Hyacinths.

Title page: Michael McKinley. A wrought iron chair adds elegance to a patio corner brightened by pelargonium, petunias, impatiens, and phaseolus (on trellis).

Gardening in Containers

The Flexibility of Container Gardens

The advantages of gardening in containers are numerous—flexibility, mobility, and compactness lead the list. Container gardens can be reshaped according to the season and the kind of plants you grow.

Annuals, Perennials, and Bulbs in Containers

In this chapter you'll find information about dozens of species and hundreds of varieties of flowering annuals and perennials, and complete instructions on how to plant and grow bulbs in containers.

Trees and Shrubs in Containers

Slow-growing or dwarf trees, shrubs, and woody vines are preferable for container growing. Here are descriptions of 50 such plants to help you make your selection.

Fruits and Vegetables in Containers

Citrus fruits, peaches, strawberries, and vegetables from beets to zucchini—even city dwellers can enjoy a bountiful harvest of container crops.

Specialty Plants for Collectors

Many container gardeners concentrate on one type of plant. If you're interested in collecting cactus, or in creating your own bonsai, here's the information to get you started.

Homemade Containers

If you'd rather make it than buy it, this chapter tells you how to build wooden containers and hanging planters of all shapes and sizes, to fit just about any location.

The Flexibility of Container Gardens

You can plant your garden in just about any kind of container. Besides the traditional clay pot and colorful ceramics, try some new ideas—pillow packs, water gardens, hanging planters—to add interest and variety to your garden.

Container gardening is more popular today than it has ever been, and with good reason. It's amazingly flexible, allowing even the urban apartment dweller to grow flowers, fruits, vegetables, vines, shrubs, and trees just about anywhere, in just about anything that will hold soil—boxes, bowls, tubs, plastic pails, garbage cans, clay pots, ceramic pots, hanging baskets, hanging bouquets, wire mesh, even outdoor carpet. This book will help you take full advantage of that flexibility to create your own container garden.

Container Gardening is full of information on how to select plants, when and how to plant them, and how to care for them. It discusses how to build, buy, and maintain containers in and around apartment houses, townhouses, roof gardens, balconies, decks, and suburban patios. It recognizes that in addition to the dedicated gardener who is interested in all areas, there are many people who

may not care about gardening as a hobby but who do enjoy the ambience and color that small trees, shrubs, and flowering plants bring to the patio, deck, or balcony.

The advantages of container gardens

Far from limiting your gardening options, container gardening extends them. Consider its flexibility, and you will see how it lends itself to limited gardening space, lack of time for gardening, frequent moves, and other aspects of modern lifestyles. Besides, container gardens have a very special, focused beauty of their own.

Containers are mobile

One advantage of container plants is that you can move them.

"As I look around the place now," says a veteran container gardener, "many a plant in a box or a tub carries me back to other homes and other people. That mugho pine in the little cedar box came from the balcony of an apartment house. It was 'loaned' to us to keep until the owners found a proper place for it. Well, I

◀

A camellia in a half-barrel and a potted chrysanthemum brighten this entryway. The azaleas will bloom later.

Geraniums, petunias, and an assortment of herbs are placed to take full advantage of the brightest spot in this Charleston courtyard.

Upper left: Ferns and asparagus ferns decorate this bright corner. Above: The cart enables this array of succulents and tender houseplants to be moved with the sun and to be taken indoors for the winter. Lower left: In autumn, chrysanthemums bloom above miniature ivy cascading from a window box. Lower center: The same window box in summer combines miniature ivy with petunias, sweet alyssum, parsley, and lettuce.

have pinched its candles to keep it small for nine years now, and it looks like it will be around for another nine years. The sago palm in the tub has traveled with us through three changes of address. We bought that dwarf spruce for an indoor Christmas tree about thirty years ago.

"Trees I planted are giving shade to others now—tree houses for children of children. I have planted many gardens. These few boxes, cans, and tubs that have traveled with me are the important plants in my garden today."

The mobility of container plants extends beyond just letting you move your plants from home to home; it also lets you display new color almost instantly, all year round. You need never have a dull season in your container garden. For example, early bulbs, flowering quince, camellias, and primroses can be moved aside as petunias, alyssum, dwarf marigolds, althea, summer vegetables, and other late-spring and summer plants come

into season. A few months later, these can be moved aside as dwarf crape myrtle and chrysanthemums come into flower and the berries of pyracantha and cleyera color brightly. The brilliant autumn foliage of dogwood, Japanese maple, and Washington thorn can color the late-season garden, and those plants bearing bright berries dress up the garden well into winter, backed up by such dependable evergreens as Japanese black pine, holly, and Carolina cherry laurel.

Gardening above the ground

A special advantage of containers is that they enable you to enjoy plants where a "dirt garden" would be impossible—on pavement, a rooftop, a balcony, an outside stairway, even a fire escape. Because they don't have to be anchored in the ground, container gardens flourish wherever adequate light and access for watering and fertilizing make them possible. If you have only a tenth-floor balcony

or a postage-stamp concrete courtyard, bring it to life with container plants. There is no reason why you shouldn't look out onto lush shrubs and trees and bright flowers, or why you can't enjoy homegrown fruit and vegetables, as long as your garden spot receives enough light. The only limitation to container gardening high above the ground is weight— bear in mind that a newly watered container, particularly a big one holding a tree, is very heavy.

The typical container garden, especially on a balcony or in a modern courtyard, has to be small. There isn't enough room to create a parklike look. But that's no real limitation. Concentrate instead on suggesting a landscape, simplifying the intricacies of nature. For centuries Japanese gardeners have been masters of this art. Capturing the spirit of nature— of the forest, the high country, or the seashore—is perhaps easier for the container gardener in miniature than for the landscape gardener on a large scale. A well-placed small rock or two, some moss, and a small piece of driftwood can create an environment that will complement and enhance your choice of container plants. As one such gardener says, "Our first step toward the Japanese garden came after we bought a hibachi. It looked so dinky—rather silly, really—up near the barbecue area. So we framed a small square in the ground just off the patio and paved it. On this we put two lava rocks (we shopped around for mossy ones) and into it we sank a gallon can of mondo grass. Now the hibachi sits framed as important as you please."

Another gardener relates: "I planted a cool, shaded miniforest in a large shallow container right outside the kitchen window. I began with a dwarf pine and a ground cover of miniature mint. I surrounded the pine with feathery club moss and one dwarf fern."

Whether you choose to plant in the style of the Japanese or not, it's worthwhile acknowledging and making use of their basic contribution— setting off plants, singly or in natural groupings. By arranging a stage for a few choice plants in the part of the garden you use most often, you get the greatest effect for the least amount of time, energy, and money.

In the spotlight

Setting a stage for container plants enhances the beauty of each plant, and its beauty is also enhanced by the very fact that it is in a container. When you put a plant in a box, tub, or pot you immediately give it a new character; it stops being a mere bush and becomes an individual shrub with its own distinction. It is "spotlighted."

As you work with plants close up in pots, boxes, and tubs, you learn to really look at them. Their individual structure and character become more important. Simply going down to the nursery and looking at the most common plants with an eye to placing them in containers can change your whole idea of how to use them. Plants seem to have both a garden personality and a container personality. For example, when a low-growing juniper is hugging the ground, it's just a ground cover—but when it's elevated in a box, pinched and pruned for a wind-swept look, it becomes a work of art.

Plants in containers can be trained into new growth patterns. A clematis that will climb 15 feet or more can

The mixed border of this penthouse garden grows entirely in containers.

This rhododendron will grow for decades in its oriental pot.

Baby's-breath, fern, and ivy make a lush setting for an oriental fountain.

be shaped as a 3-foot-wide umbrella above a 12-inch pot. Ivy can follow a curved wire, drape with simple grace, or grow as a formal column. The geranium usually looks as though it belongs on a kitchen windowsill, but trained as a standard—a patio tree— it becomes elegant and formal.

Cucumbers grow so fast that watching them form on a hanging vine can almost be a spectator sport. If you don't want a strong vining type in an elevated container, you might try planting one of the bush-type cucumbers, such as 'Patio Pik', in an 18- to 24-inch box.

Even in a sheltered corner, the gardenia standard must be protected by staking and tying.

A shrub or small tree, spotlighted by being set apart in a container, is often especially striking if it is shaped—pinched and trimmed to accentuate its natural shape, or pruned into a formal topiary. Not every shrub or tree adapts readily to container growing; in general those of formal character are easier to handle. For example, the classic sweet bay and the dwarf forms of the Carolina cherry laurel can be clipped and sheared into all sorts of formal shapes.

A small tree or a shrub doesn't have to be shaped formally to add beauty to your container garden, however. In any climate where azaleas and rhododendrons are grown, a tree worth special attention is sourwood. Slow growing in a container, it may reach 10 feet in five years. Its leaves, which resemble those of the mountain laurel, are bronzy in early spring, rich green in summer, orange and scarlet in fall. The summer show of creamy white bell-shaped flowers in 10-inch-long clusters is followed by green seed capsules in the fall. The seeds hang down from the tips of the branches, and their color changes from green to silvery gray in winter. Allowed to maintain its natural shape, and surrounded at its base by an evergreen ground cover like needlepoint ivy, this tree is a living testament to the fact that container planting sets any plant apart to make it a garden star—in this case a year-round star.

The "holding ground"

Because every plant in a container is spotlighted, a planter of perennials out of bloom, a pot of bulbs whose flowering has ended and leaves are beginning to wither, or a boxed shrub just pruned radically can stand out glaringly in a container garden. So it's a good idea to establish a "holding ground," even if it's just the least-visible corner of a balcony, where plants can stay until they are ready to return to a focal spot. Some gardening specialists—orchid growers, for instance—move flowering plants out of the greenhouse into living areas of the house, then back to the greenhouse as blossoms fade. They and all other container gardeners enjoy a distinct advantage over gardeners whose plants are established in the ground.

The holding ground can be espe-cially useful for reviving tired annuals. Remember that the life objective of all plants is to produce seeds. With annuals this must be accomplished in a single growing season. Fading flowers signal the beginning of seed production. At this time, much of the plant's energy is diverted from the production of new stems, leaves, and flowers and channeled instead into seed formation. To ensure the plant's ability to produce new flowers, remove the fading flowers by pinching or cutting them back ½ to 1 inch below the old flower head. If your plant has more seed pods than flowers, don't throw it away. Move it to the holding ground. Cut it back, fertilize and water it, and watch it start all over again. Plants such as petunias, snapdragons, and verbena, among others, respond well to this drastic treatment.

Your neighborhood nursery can also serve as a holding ground. Instead of monopolizing precious space for the long process of propagation, you can buy plants just as they are coming into bloom, so that your flower containers are always filled with blossoms and on display. When you buy a fibrous begonia in bloom, you have a flower that is 16 weeks from seed. You save weeks of growing time with many of the most useful plants: ageratum, 12 weeks; browallia, 12; coleus, 10; geranium, 16; impatiens, 12; lobelia, 12; nierembergia, 12; petunia, 12 to 15; snapdragon, 14; and thunbergia, 12 to 16.

When they are in flower at the nursery, choose from among the many favorites of the season. Try the 'Imperial Blue' pansy, an All-American bronze medal winner. Everything the catalogs write about it is true: it blooms from late winter into the summer, and takes the hot weather wonderfully. The color is a clear light blue, with contrasting bluish violet faces and a gold eye. Combine the 'Imperial Blue' in hanging bouquets with alyssum 'Tiny Tim', and plant it in wide, shallow containers with the golden-yellow face-less pansy, 'Golden Champion'.

The Madagascar periwinkle, sold as *Vinca rosea*, more correctly *Catharanthus roseus*, is a summer favorite. This weather-proof plant looks fresh and clean in the hottest weather and stays that way all summer long. As a potted plant it grows to about 10 inches tall and as wide.

Plants for shady areas

Most of the plants mentioned so far like the sun, but the mobility of containers offers a solution to the problem of shade as well, especially as trees around the garden mature and cast heavier shadows.

A patio area may receive a combination of shade and partial shade, but very little full sun during most of the year. Such an area might receive the early morning and late afternoon sun during the summer months, and reflected light from a white wall throughout the year. Because different kinds of plants grow and flower in varying degrees of shade, container plants offer a sensible way of managing a patio shade garden. This system lets you move the least shade-tolerant plants to the spot receiving the most light to increase flowering; then, when flowering begins, you can set them back in the shade. As seasonal light patterns shift, you can move container plants to areas of maximum brightness.

In thinking about shade you must consider the summer climate of your garden. If cloud cover or fog allows only filtered sunshine, anything less than full exposure is risky. However, if the sun shines almost daily and temperatures climb, many sun plants will welcome some shade.

The newer varieties of impatiens are among the best performers in the shade. These excellent container plants will bloom outdoors all summer; then you can cut them back and bring them into the house for winter color.

In addition to shade-tolerant color producers such as ageratum, browallia, begonias (fibrous and tuberous), forget-me-not, fuchsia, lobelia, and nicotiana, consider shade plants with leaf color that outshines many of the flower plants, such as the fancy-leafed caladium and coleus.

The single-colored and variegated forms of coleus are available in many sizes, leaf forms, and leaf variegations. Plants in the Carefree series are bushy, dwarfed, and well branched, with small narrow leaves 1 to 1½ inches long. Grown from seed and sold as bedding plants and in pots, they remain bushy in a container outdoors or indoors with a minimum of pinching back.

Research with cutting-grown variegated coleus shows that the leaf color of a plant varies with changes in temperature and day length. In short days and low temperatures, the leaves become narrow and the color is restricted to an area surrounding the midrib. The ideal temperature for coleus is about 70°F during the day and 62°F at night, with a 16-hour day.

Ground rules for container culture

Container plants have different soil, water, fertilizer, and cultural requirements than plants in the ground. Once you understand these requirements, they are easy to meet. Meeting them will assure you of a container garden that gives you constant satisfaction.

Container mixes

A special soil mix is necessary, according to most commercial growers of container plants and according to hundreds of thousands of successful home gardeners who have bought and used a container mix. Garden stores and nurseries sell special container mixes under a wide variety of trade names—Redi-Earth, Jiffy Mix, Metro Mix, Super Soil, Pro-Mix, and many others. Just because they are known as "soilless mixes" or "synthetic soils" doesn't mean they're artificial. In fact, they contain only natural ingredients.

The organic part of the mix may be peat moss, redwood sawdust, shavings, hardwood bark, fir bark, pine bark, or a combination of any two. The mineral part may be vermiculite, perlite, pumice, builder's sand, granite sand, or a combination of any two or three. The most commonly used minerals are vermiculite (Terralite), perlite (sponge rock), and fine sand.

When mined, *vermiculite* resembles mica. Under heat treatment, the mineral flakes expand with air spaces to 20 times their original thickness. Water is retained in the granules of vermiculite.

When mined, *perlite* is a granite-like volcanic material. When it is crushed and heat treated (at 1500° to 2000°F), it pops like popcorn and expands to twenty times its original volume. Unlike vermiculite, perlite retains water around the granules rather than in them; therefore it dries out faster than vermiculite.

Many kinds of *sand* are available,

Soil mix ingredients

Peat moss

Redwood soil conditioner

Fir bark

Vermiculite

Perlite

Sand

Good soil drainage

The ideal soil has a combination of the good points of both clay and sand, retaining moisture and at the same time allowing a constant flow of air through the soil. In packed soil, individual, unaggregated particles are compressed into a solid mass. Cultivation and the addition of organic matter aggregate the particles into porous crumbs or granules with space for air and water.

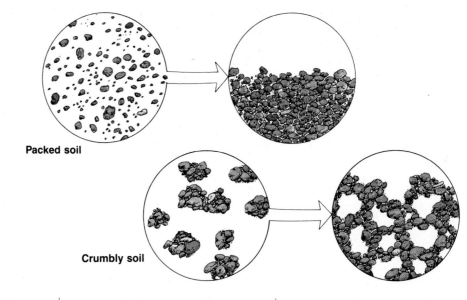

Packed soil

Crumbly soil

but for gardening washed and screened quartz sand is superior. Coarse sand is preferred for its aerating qualities. Unscreened sand contains a range of particle sizes and does not aerate as well. Sand is commonly used as a component of container soil mixes, and also to root cuttings.

The mix you buy may be half peat moss and half vermiculite, or half ground bark and half fine sand, or some other combination of the organic and mineral components. The ingredients in the mixes vary, but the principle behind all mixes is the same. Soilless "soil" must provide:

■ Fast drainage of water through the soil.
■ Air in the soil after drainage.
■ A reservoir of water in the soil after drainage.

Most important in any container mix is the air left in the soil after drainage. Plant roots require air for growth and respiration. In a heavy garden soil there is little pore space between soil particles. When water is applied to the soil it drives out air by filling the small pore spaces.

A container mix has both small and large pores (micropores and macropores). When the mix is irrigated water is held in the micropores but quickly drains through the macropores, allowing air to follow.

Aeration requirements of various plants. Plants vary greatly in their aeration requirements (percentage of air space in the soil after water from an irrigation has drained away). For example, azaleas and some ferns have very high aeration requirements. Commercial growers often grow them in straight coarse peat moss to get this

high aeration. Begonia, gardenia, podocarpus, rhododendron, snapdragon, and most foliage plants require high aeration. Intermediate aeration is best for camellia, chrysanthemum, and poinsettia. Low aeration is sufficient for carnation, geranium, ivy, and most conifers.

Drainage. Many plants will grow in a garden soil through which the water drains as slowly as 1/2 inch an hour. In a container, however, a drainage rate of 5 inches per hour is considered minimum.

Water moves by continuous capillary action through soil in the same way that it moves through a blotter. Porous material—gravel or air bubbles—will break that continuity,

and water will build up wherever the continuity is broken. A drop of water needs another drop of water behind it to drip out of a pot or into a layer of gravel. How much air is left in the soil after drainage is very important to the plant's growth. The percentage of air in soil is less by volume in a 3-inch pot than in a 6-inch pot.

Making your own mix

If you plan to do a lot of container gardening and to use large containers for shrubs and trees, you might want to make your own mix rather than buying a prepared commercial mix.

As a home gardener, you will rarely need large quantities of a mix designed for seedlings and small pots.

Water retention and air space after drainage

Although water retention doesn't vary a great deal among materials discussed here, the residual air space does. Remember that without sufficient air around the roots, most plants will suffocate. This table shows the physical properties of some mixes and the materials that go into them in terms of drainage, reservoir of water, and air after drainage. The figures indicate percent by volume.

Material	Water retention	Air space after drainage
Clay loam	54.9	4.7
Sphagnum peat moss	58.8	25.4
Fine sand	38.7	5.9
Redwood sawdust	49.3	27.9
Perlite, 1/16″–3/16″	47.3	29.8
Vermiculite, 0–3/16″	53.0	27.5
Fir bark, 0–1/8″	38.0	31.5
1:1, fine sand: fir bark	37.4	15.2
1:1, fine sand: peat moss	47.3	9.4
1:1, perlite: peat moss	51.3	23.6

When you need only a few cubic feet of container "soil," a commercial mix is your best bet. If you need more soil than that, however, you can blend these components to get 1 cubic yard (27 cubic feet, or 22 bushels) of very lightweight mix for seedlings and pots. (If you need only a small quantity of soil mix, but still want to mix it yourself, a good approximation would be to substitute half gallons for cubic feet and ounces for pounds in the following formulas.)

9 cubic feet peat moss	5 pounds 5–10–10 fertilizer
9 cubic feet vermiculite	5 pounds ground limestone
9 cubic feet perlite	

For a slightly heavier mix for seedlings and pots, try this:

14 cubic feet peat moss	5 pounds 5–10–10 fertilizer
7 cubic feet fine sand	8 pounds ground limestone
7 cubic feet perlite	

For indoor foliage plants, try this mix:

14 cubic feet peat moss	5 pounds 5–10–10 fertilizer
7 cubic feet vermiculite	1 pound iron sulphate
7 cubic feet perlite	8 pounds ground limestone

For shrubs and trees, use:

18 cubic feet ground bark or nitrogen-stabilized sawdust	5 pounds 5–10–10 fertilizer
9 cubic feet fine sand	7 pounds ground limestone
	1 pound iron sulphate

or

9 cubic feet fine sand	5 pounds 5–10–10 fertilizer
9 cubic feet peat moss	7 pounds ground limestone
9 cubic feet ground bark	1 pound iron sulphate

All of these formulas use a 5–10–10 fertilizer mix instead of combination superphosphate, calcium, or potassium nitrate in the amounts called for in Cornell Bulletin #43 (see page 12). Check the bulletin if you wish to duplicate their procedure in producing these mixes.

Tips on homemade mixes. If you want to make your own mix, choose the ingredients that will give you the blend appropriate to your planting program. If your containers receive frequent spring and fall rains, use perlite rather than vermiculite. If your mix is to be used for shrubs and trees, use a combination of ⅓ sand and ⅔ ground bark or peat moss.

The mixing process is the same for all formulas. To make a cubic yard of mix, take one of the recommended recipes; or use this even more basic one:

14 cubic feet peat moss, nitrogen-stabilized fir bark, or pine bark

14 cubic feet vermiculite or perlite

Dump the ingredients in a pile and mix them roughly. Dampen the mix as you go. Dry peat moss is much easier to wet with warm water than with cold.

Spread these fertilizer elements over the rough mix:

5 pounds ground limestone

5 pounds 5–10–10 fertilizer

Read the label. In addition to nitrogen, fertilizer should contain phosphorus and potash (potassium), limestone, and the minor elements calcium, magnesium, sulphur, iron, manganese, zinc, copper, and boron.

Use a scoop shovel to layer the ingredients into a pile. To mix thoroughly, turn the pile three times, or until it's uniformly mixed.

If you don't intend to use the mix soon after making it, store it in plastic bags or plastic garbage cans. To mix smaller quantities, reduce the amounts of the ingredients proportionately.

One cubic yard equals 27 cubic feet, or 22 bushels. However, 15 to 20 percent shrinkage occurs in mixing because of loss of air space. For 1 full yard of mix, use an additional 4 bushels, or 5 cubic feet. To obtain 1 full yard of mix, use 32 cubic feet, or 26 bushels.

Recycling waste products. Synthetic mixes may use organic ingredients that once were classed as waste products—fir bark, pine bark, and redwood sawdust—as long as nitrogen is added to compensate for nitrogen consumed by the beneficial microorganisms that cause these waste products to decay. (Routine fertilizing with a complete fertilizer should compensate for nitrogen loss.) These particular ingredients have been thoroughly tested for toxicity, pH reaction, and uniformity. Other waste products may also be used. The fewer green materials you burn or bury, the more waste products you will have for use. You might explore your area for specialized waste products—nut shells, or grape pomace where grapes are pressed.

Homemade mixes

Gather all the ingredients you need.

Measure the basic ingredients into a pile, dampen, and mix.

Spread fertilizer over the pile.

Mix the pile thoroughly.

"What comes out of the soil should go back into the soil," say conservationists. But gardeners don't always agree. While it's true that crushed almond shells, or composted grape pomace can be used safely as a soil amendment, walnut leaves and crushed walnut shells will poison the soil for garden plants. Sunflower seed hulls look promising, but tests have proven that they contain some growth-inhibiting properties. Any organic material, especially agricultural by-products, must be tested carefully to be sure that it contains no toxic elements.

Keeping it simple. Some gardeners believe that every type of plant requires a special soil mix and like to work out complicated mixes of five or six ingredients. They just won't accept the fact that a simple combination of peat moss and vermiculite, or perlite, or fine sand, can be used with almost all types of plants, from cacti to tropicals, with only some modification of watering routines according to the needs of the individual plant.

This doesn't mean that you shouldn't tamper with the mix you buy. On the contrary—if the mix is so lightweight that the container will tip over in a slight wind, by all means add sand. Some gardeners, unwilling to leave well enough alone, add garden topsoil to the mix when planting in containers. But when you add soil you lose all the advantages of a sterilized mix. For example, if you are growing container tomatoes in a soilless mix to avoid soil-borne tomato diseases, it would hardly pay to add garden soil—that would amount to inviting the same diseases you are trying to stave off.

The standard soilless mixes are free of disease organisms, weed seeds, and insects. All the nutrients needed for initial plant growth are usually included in the mix. The soilless mixes are ready for immediate use. If you bring home a 2-cubic-foot bag, you will have enough "soil" for 20 to 22 gallon-sized containers, or 35 to 40 pots 6 inches deep. You'll need 4 cubic feet for a planter box 24″ × 36″ × 8″ deep.

The light weight of Jiffy Mix and other peat moss/vermiculite mixes comes in handy when it's time to move containers from one spot to another, or when your "patio" is a roof or balcony, where weight can be a problem. Jiffy Mix weighs less than half as much as garden soil when both are soaked.

Converting garden soil into container soil. When keeping the container soil sterile isn't so important—for example, when you are planting most shrubs and trees—you may find it cheaper and more practical to condition garden soil and have it on hand for container use than to create an artificial soil mix every time you plant a container.

To condition garden soil, you can add all types of organic material—peat moss, ground bark, manure, leaf mold, and compost, in all stages of decay. All organic materials help make heavy soils more friable and sandy soils better able to retain water and nutrients. Manure and compost perform the additional service of increasing the fertility of the soil. If you're using organic amendments such as these, or organic mulches of leaves, straw, or grass clippings, it's a good idea to add organic matter to the soil every year to replace that which has broken down.

Since the purpose of adding organic matter is to change the physical structure of the soil, adding a little dab of this or that won't do the job—a little peat moss or a little straw added to compressed clay soil makes a good adobe brick. Instead, top garden soil with a 2-inch layer of ground bark, rototill it into the top 2 inches of soil, and you'll have a really useful container soil. Water will drain through it rapidly; it will have the right amount of air space after irrigation; and it will retain water sufficiently for good plant growth. Once you have created conditioned soil, you can transfer it from ground to container as needed.

For more information. If you wish to dig deeper into the subject of soil mixes for growing plants in containers, this publication will be helpful:

Cornell Peat-Lite Mixes for Commercial Plant Growing. Information Bulletin 43, by James W. Boodley and Raymond Sheldrake, Jr. Send $1.00 to Cornell Distribution Center, 7 Research Park, Ithaca, NY 14850.

Using fertilizer properly

You need to pay closer attention to plants growing in containers than to the same plants growing in a flower border or in a vegetable patch. Because of the limited volume in a container the soil dries out faster than in the garden, so you must compensate for the smaller root area by watering and feeding more frequently.

If you are using a mix containing a 5–10–10 fertilizer, normally you should begin applying more fertilizer three weeks after planting. If you need to water frequently after planting, start the feeding program earlier.

Because watering leaches fertilizers out of the mix, how often you water determines how often you should fertilize. A container garden requires more frequent watering and fertilizing than a garden in the ground. Moreover, since fertilizers will leach from mixtures containing perlite faster than from those containing vermiculite, plants grown in a peat moss/perlite mix will require even more frequent applications of fertilizer.

Some container gardeners prefer to fertilize with a weak nutrient solution, applying it with every other irrigation. If you choose this method, use only 1/5 the amount of fertilizer called for on the label for a monthly application. That is, if the label calls for 1 tablespoon to a gallon of water, use 1 tablespoon, as specified, but increase the dilution by using 5 gallons of water.

Plants don't require a large amount of fertilizer at any one time, but they do need to be fed continually. The nutrient solution applications just described satisfy the plant's need for a constant supply of nutrients. Time-release fertilizers are another popular method of meeting this need. As the plant receives water, these fertilizers are released in small amounts. (Check the label for rate of application.) The easiest method is to use a time-release fertilizer mixed with the soil. Three-month and twelve-month release fertilizers are available. Whatever fertilizer you use, be sure it is balanced and contains the minor elements listed on page 11.

When you plant or transplant

It's best to wet a lightweight synthetic mix before using it—a pot filled with dry mix is difficult to wet properly. The easiest and least messy way is to add water directly to the plastic bags the mix comes in. Hold the top of the bag and knead the water in until the mixture is evenly moist. Let the entire bag sit over-

When you bring a plant home

Make sure your nursery plants don't dry out.

Push up with thumb.

Use a putty knife to cut through soil and rootball.

Remove plants gently from containers.

Punch holes in bottom of peat pots, and remove upper edge of container or wrapping to keep plant from drying out.

night before using to ensure an even distribution of moisture throughout the mixture. Then fill the container, firming the mix down, especially near the edges. Water the plants thoroughly after transplanting. If you don't plan to use all the mix immediately, keep it moist by tying the top of the bag tightly.

When you pick up plants at the nursery, chances are that they will continue to perform well if you care for them properly. Mishandling of plants most often occurs during the first few days of ownership. Here are some tips on how to handle your fresh-from-the-nursery plants.

If you run out of time to plant all your choices and must hold some

plants over for the following weekend, make sure that they don't dry out in the interim. Water them as you would any container plant until you are ready to remove them from the nursery containers. A damp (not wet) rootball will not shatter or stick to the edge of the container.

Plants are grown in plastic, fiber, and metal containers. Remove the plants from cell packs and market packs the easy way: squeeze the bottom of the container in the cell pack to force the rootball above the lip. When removing plants from market trays, cut the soil in blocks. Use a putty knife for cutting soil and removing the rootball. Don't pull plants out of containers.

Ask the nursery to cut straight-sided cans. Plants grown in cans, pots, or tubs with sloping sides can be tapped out of the container. Hold the container upside down and tap it against a ledge. Hold the rootball with the plant stem between your fingers.

Handle biodegradable containers carefully. Small plants may come in peat pots, Jiffy 7's, or paper pots; larger shrubs may come in fiber pots, or balled and burlapped (B&B). Plant peat pots and Jiffy 7's below the soil line. With peat pots, punch holes in the bottom and cut off the upper exposed edges of the container. The rootball dries out quickly if any part of the peat pot or wrapping remains above the soil surface.

Prune the roots when necessary. If roots have formed outside the rootball along the sides and bottom of the container prune them before setting the plant into the larger container by making three or four cuts from top to bottom with a sharp knife down the side of the rootball. The pruning will speed up the formation of new roots and the penetration of roots into the soil surrounding the rootball.

Set a root-pruned plant into the container soil at the level it grew in the nursery. Firm the soil around the rootball and water thoroughly. Keep the rootball moist until the roots have spread into the surrounding soil. Soil differences may make the rootball dry out even though the surrounding soil is wet.

Watering

After placing the plant in a container, water the soil thoroughly. After settling, the soil should be ½ to 1 inch below the rim of the can to allow *one* application of water to moisten the rootball and drain through the container. If the watering space is too shallow, you may have to water, let it drain into the soil, and then water again.

It's advisable to use a mulch of bark chunks, pea gravel, or marble chips, or a ground cover such as alyssum, ajuga, or vinca over the soil in a large container. This will dress up the planting and slow down evaporation, and also keep the planting soil from being disturbed when you water.

How frequently you should water depends on the soil mix; the type and size of container; temperature; wind; sunlight; and humidity.

Some plants advertise their need for water by wilting quite drastically. But once watered, many of them—impatiens, strawberries, and tomatoes, for instance—make an equally dramatic and speedy recovery.

Don't water by the calendar. A plant that needs water every day during a stretch of warm sunny days can go on an every-other-day schedule in cloudy weather. One of the great values of the synthetic soil mixes is that they can't become waterlogged if the container drains properly.

A plant in a porous clay pot will need water more frequently than one in a plastic or glazed pot. Some gardeners solve the evaporation problem by placing the pot inside a larger pot and insulating the space between the

When you plant

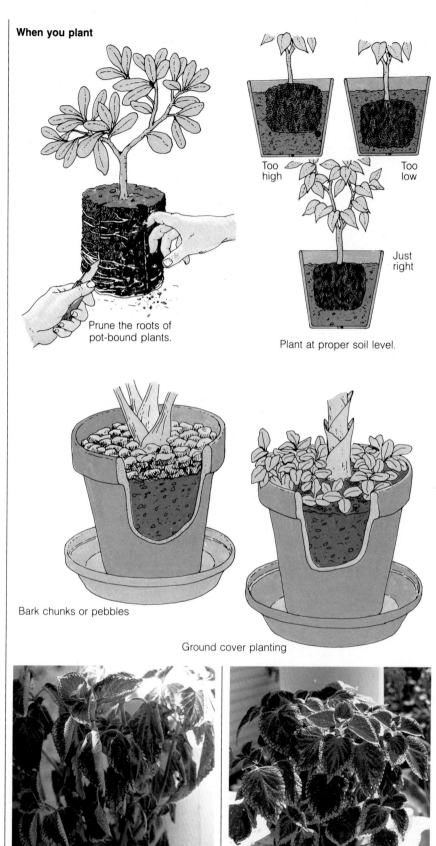

Prune the roots of pot-bound plants.

Too high

Too low

Just right

Plant at proper soil level.

Bark chunks or pebbles

Ground cover planting

After it was placed in the shade and watered thoroughly, this wilted coleus revived within an hour.

Watering

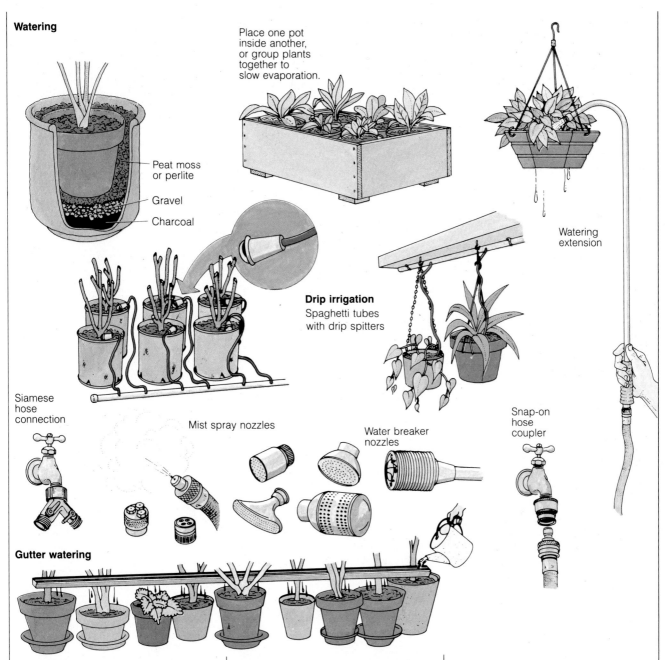

Place one pot inside another, or group plants together to slow evaporation.

Peat moss or perlite

Gravel

Charcoal

Watering extension

Drip irrigation
Spaghetti tubes with drip spitters

Siamese hose connection

Mist spray nozzles

Water breaker nozzles

Snap-on hose coupler

Gutter watering

two with peat moss or perlite and layers of charcoal and/or gravel. If you do this be careful not to over-water, or the insulation will become soaked.

One way to solve the evaporation problem with small pots is to group them together in a wooden box. A 14″ × 24″ × 10″ deep box will hold two 5-gallon containers, or a group of 6-inch pots. Put ground bark or peat moss around the pots for insulation and as a mulch.

Watering devices can make life easier for the container gardener. The Siamese hose connector with double shut-offs lets you set up a permanent watering system for containers without having to fiddle with hose bibs.

Drip-irrigation hardware permits

many types of container-watering systems. Here, a length of plastic pipe with a half-dozen spaghetti tubes with drip spitters attached delivers the small but constant amount of water the containers need. It's one way to "vacationize" your garden.

Mist spray nozzles can give container plants the fog they need on hot dry days.

The water extension makes it easy to water hanging baskets.

The water breaker delivers a high volume of water without disturbing the soil in the container.

To water many pots at one time, you can use a length of roof gutter as the water distributor. The gutter is closed at both ends. Punch holes in the gutter, spacing them to water

each of the pots. Advocates of this method say it's easier to fill the gutter two or three times, if necessary, than to water a dozen pots individually.

A crucial fact about watering container plants is that soil sours, roots rot, and root-killing mineral salts build up in any container that drains poorly, or that stands in its own drainage water. If a container is in a saucer, empty the saucer after every watering. If the container is too heavy to lift, empty the saucer with a turkey baster. Unless you can empty the attached saucer of a hanging planter after every watering, remove the saucer permanently. If a container drains slowly, more or larger drainage holes, or a faster-draining mix, or both, are needed.

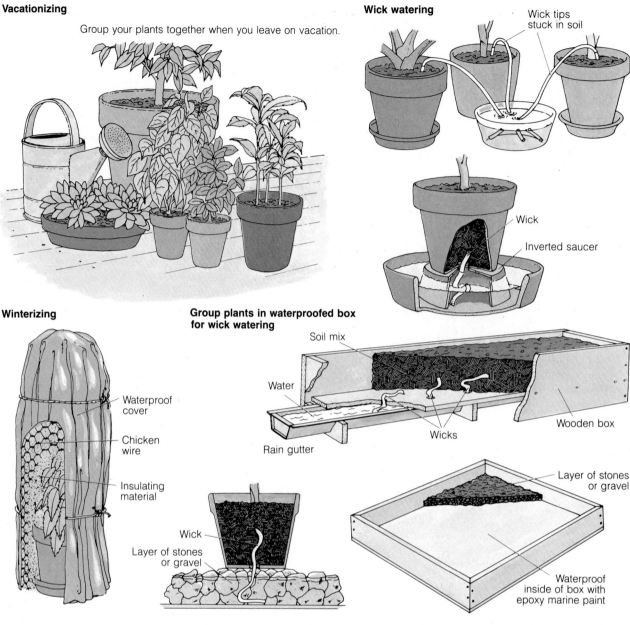

Vacationizing

Group your plants together when you leave on vacation.

Wick watering

Wick tips
stuck in soil

Wick

Inverted saucer

Winterizing

Waterproof
cover

Chicken
wire

Insulating
material

**Group plants in waterproofed box
for wick watering**

Soil mix

Water

Wicks

Rain gutter

Wooden box

Wick

Layer of stones
or gravel

Layer of stones
or gravel

Waterproof
inside of box with
epoxy marine paint

Vacationizing

Can your plants get along without you for a long weekend? For a week? Regardless of which watering system you use—automatic, drip, or wick— a plant sitter or at least an occasional visit from a friendly neighbor is a necessity if you plan to be away for a week or more. Even the most sophisticated watering systems need attention. However, you can make the plant sitter's watering job less burdensome in several ways.

Move the containers into a single watering spot, where they will be protected from the wind and direct sun. Sun-loving plants can take filtered shade for a week or two.

Wick watering can take care of containers for a week or more. Put one end of the wick in a pail of water

and the other in the soil of the container. This will give the container a continuous supply of water. You can use a wick of glass wool, fraying the end that goes into the soil, or a nylon clothesline. Special wicks are also available.

You can build a two-compartment planter box that can be watered and fed with wicks. The upper compartment holds the soil and plants; the lower compartment has a metal gutter that holds water with a nutrient solution for wick watering and feeding the plants.

To create a water reservoir for a number of wick-watered pots, you can use large custom-made pans of sheet metal, or homemade wooden boxes made watertight and filled with gravel.

Winterizing

Winterizing is an important consideration if you live in a cold-winter climate. It can make the difference between survival and death for your container plants. You can protect even the most vulnerable plant from the cold by wrapping plant and container in a chicken-wire cylinder, filling the cylinder with insulating material such as hay, straw, or dried leaves, and keeping it dry with a waterproof cover.

Don't remove this covering too soon in spring—frost damage can occur when balmy days are followed by cold windy nights.

If your winters are less severe but still cold, make the most of the containers' mobility and move them to protected areas during cold weather.

Moving heavy containers

The use of a lightweight soil mix—peat moss and perlite or vermiculite—lessens the weight problem, but a moist mix still weighs far more than a dry one.

For moving large, heavy tubs, a dolly on casters is a welcome aid. In fact, it pays to attach a set of casters to the base of any large box or tub. Casters make the container easier to move, and they also create air space beneath the container, robbing earwigs and slugs of a potential hiding place.

If you have a great many containers, you'll find a handtruck to be a useful gadget. Attaching a trash bag to the handtruck lightens the chore of garden cleanup.

Protecting container bottoms

If the bottom of a wooden container is in direct contact with a moist surface eventually it, and maybe the surface too, will rot. All planters, tubs, and boxes should have air space beneath them. If the box or tub you buy or build doesn't have casters or feet, use small wooden blocks to keep the container an inch or so above ground. Elevating a container often has the additional benefit of keeping drainage holes from blocking.

You can treat wooden containers inside and at the bottom with a wood preservative containing copper sulfate, such as Cuprinol or Copper Green. Paint it on with brush or spray. Do not use creosote or wood preservatives containing penta-chlorophenol, such as Wood Life or Penta-treat—they are toxic to plants. When treating exterior plywood, remember to seal the edges.

Pest control for container gardens

Just because plants are in containers doesn't mean they are immune from insect damage. As one experienced gardener says, "Container gardens have many advantages, but they may also invite such pests as slugs, snails, earwigs, and sow bugs. The moist atmosphere of the containers offers a haven, like an oasis on the desert, to these moisture-seeking pests. Instead of sprinkling bait on the soil in the pot, which may attract slugs or snails to the pot, place some pellets on a fresh, damp lettuce leaf and set it near the pot to lure the pest from the pot to the ground. Do this in

If your planter is too heavy to lift

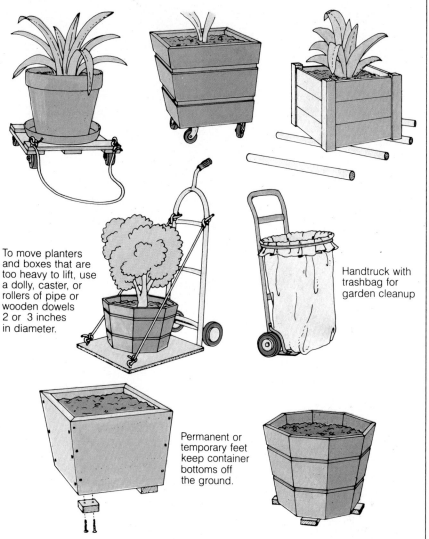

To move planters and boxes that are too heavy to lift, use a dolly, caster, or rollers of pipe or wooden dowels 2 or 3 inches in diameter.

Handtruck with trashbag for garden cleanup

Permanent or temporary feet keep container bottoms off the ground.

the early evening after wetting the area around and underneath the containers. The following morning it's easy to pick up your "catch" and dump it in the trash. Repeat the procedure for three consecutive evenings, then again about every ten days until the problem is eliminated.

"Earwig bait should be handled in the same manner. Additional baiting can be effective for earwigs by providing some rolled-up newspaper that holds some bait for any daytime munchers. They normally hide during the daylight hours, and the darkness of the rolled-up news-papers is an attraction for them."

Because container plants must be watered frequently, you'll be inspecting them frequently, which means that you'll have a good chance of noticing and dealing with the initial insect attack before it gets out of hand. In fact, if container garden maintenance can be summed up in one rule, that rule is to inspect your plants regularly and frequently. With experience, you will be able not only to spot immediate problems, like earwigs, but more insidious problems like a nutritional deficiency or the need for a lighter soil mix.

Pest Control

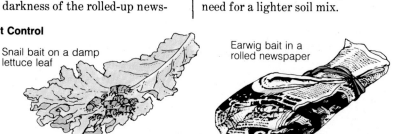

Snail bait on a damp lettuce leaf

Earwig bait in a rolled newspaper

Three special kinds of containers

Here are ideas for three specialized types of containers that can be combined with more conventional pots and tubs of soil to extend the dimensions, variety, and beauty of your container garden. The first offers a simple means of having plants in even the most difficult spots; the second allows you to create an outstanding garden feature with unusual plants; and the third helps you to get your container garden off the ground—literally.

Pillow packs

A pillow pack is a seasonal container made by filling a "pillow" with synthetic soil mix and planting it so that flowers and foliage hide the pack itself. The result is a dense mass of vegetation, from a single plant or a whole bed, in a flexible container. The pillow pack can be molded like putty to fit an odd-shaped cranny or to nestle securely on a surface too sloping or uneven to support a conventional planter. It is clean, it provides maximum space for soil and roots in a confined spot, and its soil stays put, even in a heavy wind.

A large pack, or a group of packs, can be placed in the corner of a balcony or small patio to form a mound of blossom and foliage, softening the harsh angles of the planting area and suggesting the contours of a natural landscape. Packs can be used alone or in combination with pots, tubs, and boxes. Packs of various sizes can be placed in decorative planters, and they can be transferred easily from one planter to another to create new displays.

Ordinary kitchen-type plastic bags—vegetable bags, refrigerator bags, bread bags, or trash bags—are potential pillow packs to be filled with lightweight synthetic soil. Or you can buy plastic tubes at a plastic supply shop. One of the simplest pillow packs comes ready-made: an unopened bag of commercial planting mix.

To make the pillow pack, fill the bag or tube with the synthetic soil mix to within 2 or 3 inches of the top. Fold the plastic at each end and sew or staple the ends closed. Slit the plastic where the seedlings are to be inserted. To make watering easier, insert small

These pillow packs of petunias should be removed from their decorative containers for watering.

Planting a pillow pack

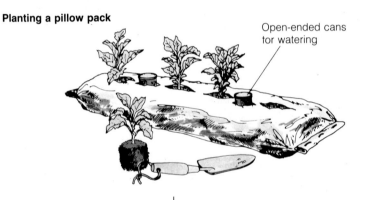

Open-ended cans for watering

open-ended cans, such as frozen juice cans with both ends cut out. Use one or two cans in a small pillow, or one can about every 18 inches in a long tube. Punch small holes in the bottom for drainage. After the plants have been in about three weeks, start a liquid feeding program.

Water gardens

Gertrude Jekyll, the famous English garden designer, considered water the "soul of the garden." Although she was writing about in-ground gardens, there is no reason why you can't introduce the special beauty of water to your balcony, deck, or patio container garden. You can create a large water garden that delights the eye with its beauty and the ear with the sound of moving water, or you can work on a smaller scale with a portable plastic tub only 2 feet in diameter. Even the smallest pool creates a magical focal point. A small plastic pool can be placed inside a more decorative container, such as a half wine barrel, with heavy casters for greater mobility. Grow your water

plants in gallon-size plastic or clay pots and arrange them in the tub at the varying heights.

Hardy water lilies. Carol and Bill Uber, water-gardening experts and owners of Van Ness Water Gardens (2460 North Euclid Avenue, Upland, California 91786), offer these tips on the care of hardy water lilies.

"In frost-free areas, plant hardy water lilies any time from February through October. Once roots have established, lilies will winter over safely in the pool as long as the roots don't freeze. In cold-winter areas, plant water lilies any time from April through August, when there is no danger of freezing. Except in the coldest climates lilies will winter over in the pool if you cover the pool with boards and straw. If your winter climate is so cold that this method won't keep the pool from freezing solid, lift the pots of lilies after the first frost, when the foliage has begun to die back, and store the pots in a cool cellar. Keep the soil moist, or dry rot will attack the roots."

In his book *The Lotus Book of Water*

Gardening, author Bill Heritage says of the hardy water lilies, "The elegant, almost exotic, beauty of water lilies creates the impression that they must surely need much expertise to grow, and coddling to survive the rigors of winter. In fact they require no winter protection whatever throughout Britain and in most parts of North America. Their constitutions, far from being delicate, are robust enough to survive considerable abuse.

"The hardy water lilies are perennial; growth disappears each autumn and is renewed every spring, year after year. They dislike shade, violent currents, and cold mains or spring water. All they need to flower abundantly summer after summer is correct planting, a comfortable depth of water for the variety, and a place in the sun. The more sun you give them the more flowers they'll give you."

Tropical water lilies. Set out the tender tropical lilies only after nights are warm—May 15 to September 30, depending on your location. According to the Ubers, "In mild climates [tropical water lilies] may be left in the pool all winter. We do not guarantee them to live over, but almost without exception they do in mild-winter areas. In moderately cold high-altitude areas you can leave lilies in the pool and cover it securely with clear fiberglass. In May, get in and see that the bulbs are ½ inch under the soil, and crown (rough) side up. In colder climates, take the bulbs out after the lilies have gone dormant. Store them in a can of moist sand in a frost-free cellar or garage until May, then plant them. Tropicals have so many blooms and are so beautiful they are worth this little extra work."

The edibles. You can grow a variety of edible water plants in one tub. For a substantial harvest, use a container the size of a half wine barrel. A 25-gallon container will yield approximately the following crops, according to Bill Uber.

"A planting of lotus in April will produce five or six edible roots when harvested during the dormant period in October or November of the second year. The roots of the lotus can be French fried like potatoes.

"A tub of 30 to 40 Chinese water chestnuts will grow numerous sedge-like, hollow stems, to 2 feet or more, from bulbs in the first year. Then, when they're dormant, you can expect to harvest about a hundred chestnuts.

These edible water plants are (left to right) Chinese water chesnut, lotus, violet-stemmed taro, and watercress.

Clean water formula

For each square yard of surface area your water garden should contain:

Oxygenating plants: 2 bunches of 6 stems each.
Water lily: 1 medium to large plant.
Snails: 12 ramshorn or trapdoor water snails.
Fish: 2 fish, each 4 to 5 inches long.

A few from the harvest should be saved for a second-year planting.

"An early planting of five or six violet-stemmed taro (*Xanthosoma violaceum*) in April will produce 5- to 7-inch, bluish green, arrowhead-shaped leaves on violet stems about 2 feet high, then go dormant about six months later. Harvest during this dormancy will yield enough tubers for about two dishes of poi. Only the tubers are edible.

"Watercress gives an almost instant crop. Pinch off leaves and tips for a piquant salad, but leave enough stems, roots, and leaves that plants can continue to grow rapidly. Watercress grows best in cool water."

Pool balance. The Ubers have worked out an ecosystem for pool gardens in which plants, fish, and snails live in harmony to keep the pool water clean and free of insects. Four elements are needed:

1. Oxygenating plants are important for replenishing oxygen. Various species of *Elodea* (some of which have been called *Anacharis*) are best for most containers.
2. Water lilies are essential—their pads provide surface coverage, preventing loss of oxygen and keeping the water cool.
3. Snails eat algae, fish wastes, and decaying matter, which otherwise encourage algae growth.
4. Fish eat such pests as aphids, flies, mosquito larvae, and other insects. Keep in mind, however, that overfeeding fish with commercial fish food will change the water balance drastically.

Above: Hanging fuchsia 'Jack Shahan'. Above right: Hanging vegetables in this greenhouse room include tomato, pepper, and eggplant. Center right: Hanging plantings of blue and white *Campanula isophylla* are turned weekly to keep them well rounded.

Sweet alyssum, pansies, and marigolds grow with parsley and lettuce in planters and wire baskets hanging or attached to a post.

Hanging planters

Hanging planters add an interesting dimension to many landscaping situations. On decks and patios or inside such garden structures as arbors, gazebos, and pergolas, hanging planters can highlight interesting details and disguise unattractive ones. They can also help define the space visually. If they are lightweight, and they should be, they can be moved from place to place indoors or outdoors for special occasions. Where space is limited, hanging planters may be a necessity. You can accommodate many more plants by getting some of them off the floor, and also avoid the monotony of having everything on one level.

The variety of hanging planters. The simplest hanging planter is a clay or plastic pot suspended by a clamp-on wire hanger or a wire hanger attached through holes in the pot. Some commercial hangers have built-in swivels so that every side of the planter can get sun.

A hanging container needs more protection from sun and wind than it would on the ground. When the common clay pot is exposed on all sides to the movement of air it becomes an efficient evaporative unit and requires either a waterproof cover or much more frequent watering.

Many hanging planters are made of wood. The most durable are redwood or other woods that are slow to decay. Wood is relatively lightweight, and many people find it more attractive than plastic.

Container plants and wicker chairs make a Victorian solarium of this cozy sunporch.

Hanging pots

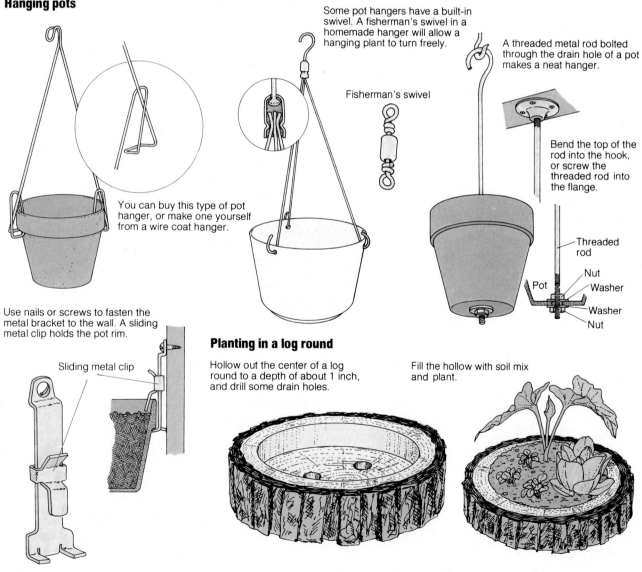

Some pot hangers have a built-in swivel. A fisherman's swivel in a homemade hanger will allow a hanging plant to turn freely.

A threaded metal rod bolted through the drain hole of a pot makes a neat hanger.

Fisherman's swivel

You can buy this type of pot hanger, or make one yourself from a wire coat hanger.

Bend the top of the rod into the hook, or screw the threaded rod into the flange.

Threaded rod

Nut

Washer

Pot

Washer

Nut

Use nails or screws to fasten the metal bracket to the wall. A sliding metal clip holds the pot rim.

Sliding metal clip

Planting in a log round

Hollow out the center of a log round to a depth of about 1 inch, and drill some drain holes.

Fill the hollow with soil mix and plant.

How to plant a plastic hanging basket

1. Make four or five 1½'' holes in the sides of the pot, either by drilling and enlarging with a hand rasp, or by burning with a hot metal pipe or soldering iron. Be sure there are drain holes in the bottom.

Plastic film

2. Cut a 3'' square of plastic film for each plant. Slip the plastic around the stems of the plants.

3. Tuck the plastic into the holes as you put the plants through. This will keep the soil from spilling out. Sphagnum moss wrapped around the stem also works well.

4. Fill the basket with soil mix and add the remaining plants to the top. Water thoroughly.

Materials needed:
10'' plastic pot
Soil mix
7 or 8 plants
Plastic film or sphagnum moss

A three-piece hanging basket

This hanging basket snaps together easily.

The upper ring

The bottom pot

The saucer

1. Fill the bottom pot with soil mix up to the slots. Lay the plants on the soil and put the stems through the slots.

2. Snap on the top ring. Fill with soil mix to within an inch or so of the rim and plant the remaining plants in the top.

3. Snap on the saucer and water thoroughly.

Planting in driftwood

Handsomely twisted driftwood or tree branches can make beautiful planters. Decide where you want your planting pocket. A concave curve or the space between two or more branches is usually the easiest and most attractive place to plant.

Materials needed:
Driftwood
Chicken wire
Galvanized fence staples (staple-gun staples will rust)
Sphagnum moss
Soil mix

1. Cut and form the wire to the shape you want and staple it securely to the wood. Leave an opening at the top for inserting the moss and soil.

2. Line the wire with sphagnum moss. Overlap the pieces so the soil can't leak out.

3. Fill the pocket with soil mix and plant. Attach a heavy-duty screw eye so you can hang your driftwood planter up.

Note: If your driftwood comes from the ocean, soak it in fresh water for several days to remove the salt before planting.

Wire baskets come in many shapes and sizes. Here's how to line them with sphagnum moss, fill them with soil, and plant them.

Immerse the sphagnum moss in a pail of water, remove it in 6-inch plugs, and squeeze out most of the water.

Squeeze the moss down around the top two wires, pushing the first piece tightly against a vertical wire.

Line the inside of the basket with large pieces of moss overlapped sufficiently to hold soil.

Trim any straggly pieces of moss off the outside, then fill the bottom with 1½ inches of moist soil.

Use your fingers from both sides to poke holes at soil level large enough to insert plants.

Insert plants with rootballs lying on soil surface, then raise the soil level and insert more plants.

Among the most useful and attractive hanging planters are moss baskets, heavy-gauge wire baskets usually lined with sphagnum moss, as illustrated on this page. A well-planted moss basket is a showy living bouquet, a solid mass of foliage and flowers on the bottom, sides, and top.

Some wire baskets are designed to be hung like pictures on wall brackets, rather than suspended. Similar to these moss baskets are hanging planters devised by stapling chicken wire to create a moss-lined planting pocket on a driftwood bracket or hanger. Also similar is the hanging

cylinder, made of heavy-gauge wire fencing and a perforated wood bottom, lined with green outdoor carpet, and planted through slits cut in the carpet. As the plants develop, the carpet nearly disappears from view.
Care of your hanging planter. However you choose to put together your

hanging planter, it's important to leave enough watering space at the top. Fill the planter with soil only up to ½ inch below the top, not up to the very top. Pack the sphagnum moss in thick and tight around the top inch of a moss basket. This creates a watering basin that allows the soil in the container to get thoroughly wet when you water, which in some cases should be daily or even twice a day. Use one heavy application of water to wet the soil, or else you'll have to keep watering in small amounts three or four times a day in order to get a good soaking.

Keeping the planter neat and in full color requires vigilant grooming. Remove all spent blooms. Prune off straying shoots. Pin shoots or vines to the moss with old-fashioned hairpins.

When frost or age has put an end to a moss basket's good looks, take it to the compost pile or the work section of the garden and turn it upside down. Peel the layer of sphagnum moss off the root ball and save the moss and the wire for later reuse. Just clean the moss of any foreign material, soil, or plant roots, and use it to build a new basket with fresh soil.

Otherwise, care of a hanging planter is the same as for any other planter, as described in the next chapter.

Choosing plants for hanging planters. The following plants have drooping or trailing growth habits suitable for hanging planters. You can read about them in the following chapters.

Bulbs: Achimenes and tuberous begonia.

Annuals and perennials: 'Sprenger' asparagus fern, aubrieta, basket-of-gold, Italian bellflower, candytuft, squirrel's-foot fern, ivy geranium, Kenilworth ivy, trailing lobelia, moneywort, dwarf periwinkle, thunbergia, and verbena.

Shrubs: Camellias 'Showa-No-Sakae' and 'Shishi Gashira', trailing cotoneaster, juniper, and lantana.

Woody vines: Dwarf bougainvillea, hanging crape myrtle, ivy, star jasmine, and wintercreeper.

Succulents: Ice plant, orchid cactus, Christmas cactus, and burro tail.

Herbs: Prostrate rosemary, oregano, and mint.

This list doesn't exhaust all the possibilities, but it does suggest some of the most dependable and graceful plants for your hanging containers.

Top: Like all asparagus ferns, *Asparagus sprengeri* lends itself to use in hanging baskets. Center left: *Asparagus meyersi.* Center right: *Thunbergia alata* and *Lobelia erinus* make a cheery window box combination. Left: This lath house provides bright, cool work space and a perfect home for ferns.

A vast array of planters

This page is devoted to a shopping guide for plant containers. Here are some of the numerous kinds of containers you'll find in garden stores; functional plastic wastebaskets, buckets, and garbage pails from supermarkets; and unusual offerings from hardware stores, import shops, and kitchen specialty stores. There's a big, varied, fascinating collection of containers to choose from. Containers are where you find them; let your imagination be your guide. Consult the chapter on "Homemade Containers" (pages 83 through 93) to learn how to construct your own.

Top: Sizes and shapes of clay pots vary enormously in a typical garden store. Center: Wood, ceramic, clay, glass, and plastic containers are widely available. Left: Clay strawberry jars are useful for growing flowers as well.

Annuals, Perennials, and Bulbs in Containers

**Your garden can be a rainbow of color all year round
when you rotate your containers and hanging baskets to
take advantage of the seasonal brilliance of spring
daffodils, summer geraniums, and autumn
chrysanthemums.**

Annuals and perennials are what most people call simply "flowers." They are the principal, and sometimes the only, plants in a typical container garden. Within a single growing season annuals sprout, mature, bloom, and die. Perennials endure season after season, some dying back to the ground and others remaining green.

Practically speaking, of course, climate determines whether certain plants are annuals or perennials. In San Francisco geranium is a perennial, but in Philadelphia it is an annual. Geranium and basket-of-gold are among the perennials listed in this chapter that are grown as annuals in cold climates. Also included are several foliage perennials, such as ivy and asparagus fern—the backbone if not the colorful stars of many container gardens.

Also discussed in this chapter are several annual and perennial vines. (In addition, some woody ones are described in the chapter "Trees and

◀

Above a bed of tulips and forget-me-nots, *Schizanthus* makes a brilliant hanging display.

Shrubs in Containers.") Before you choose a vine for your container garden, be sure of what kind of support it requires. Many vines are content just to trail, like ivy. Others, like thunbergia, are best displayed if they have a trellis to twine around. Climbing sweet pea is definitely a trellis plant.

When annuals and perennials are confined to containers, they become movable flower arrangements. You can place the plants here and there, filling empty spaces as needed with the bright colors of pansies or petunias. You can also use them to highlight other plants or garden features or to call attention to a doorway. For instance, white impatiens can help liven up a shady corner, and the bright colors of geraniums or zinnias make an entryway more inviting.

Lots of annuals and perennials perform well in the confines of a container. You'll find an extensive but by no means exhaustive list on the following pages. All plants listed here meet two basic conditions: They are generally available, and they are beautiful in containers. Because few container gardeners have the space or the inclination to fill many containers with short-season kinds of perennials

when they can enjoy colorful annuals throughout the gardening season, we have emphasized annuals, and certain perennials usually grown as annuals.

Whenever possible, the following chart indicates a plant's best use. When that use is "hanging baskets," you can usually feature the plant alone. "Hanging bouquets" means that a plant looks best tucked in among others.

Each plant is designated as a "warm-season" or a "cool-season" performer, or both. Cool-season plants are generally frost-tolerant and go to seed quickly during the summer. Most warm-season plants, however, need these long, warm days to develop fully. Warm-season annuals are usually killed by the first heavy frost.

You can grow most of these annuals and perennials from seed, but all are available as transplants—often a better idea, especially when germination and maturation take a long time. (See the columns "Days to Germination" and "Sowing to Flowering.")

Some perennials are most easily located in nurseries or catalogs by their botanical (Latin) names, so the botanical names of those are included parenthetically in the following chart.

Achimenes

White alyssum and dwarf marigolds

Name	Warm or Cool-Season Plant	Season of Bloom	Size and Form	Color	Exposure			Days to Germination	Sowing to Flowering (Weeks)	Comments	Uses
					Sun	Partial shade	Full shade				
Achimenes 'Cascade' series	W	Sp, S		Blue, pink, rose, purple, light yellow, orange, crimson	•	–	–			Plant tubers early spring. Store in cool, dry place during winter dormancy.	Hanging baskets. Plant 3 to 5 bulbs per 12″ basket, 1″ deep.
Ageratum	W	S, F	6–12″ mounds	Shades of blue, purple most useful	•	•		8	12	Can be brought indoors in fall for winter bloom.	Hanging bouquet tuck-in, or plant 3 or 4 in shallow box. Combine with marigolds or pink petunias.
'Blue Blazer'			6″	Deep blue						Compact; flowers profusely.	
'Blue Mink'			12″	Light blue						More vigorous than above. Large flower heads.	
'Blue Puffs' ('Blue Danube')			7″	Light blue						Very uniform plants.	
'Summer Snow'			6″	White						Form similar to 'Blue Blazer'.	
Alyssum	C–W	Sp, S, F	3–8″ low trailing mat	White, purple, rose	•	•		8	8	Fast-growing, tough plant. Profuse bloomer. Faintly fragrant. Will spread 10–15″.	Low growing. 'Tiny Tim' most useful in hanging bouquets. A most versatile plant. Use as ground cover in tubbed shrub or tree.
'Carpet of Snow'			4″	White						Forms very dense carpet of flowers.	
'Tiny Tim'			2–3″	White						Early flowering miniature.	
'Rosie O'Day' (AAS)			4″	Deep rose						Retains deep color well.	
'Royal Carpet' (AAS)			3–5″	Violet-purple						Profuse flowers.	
'Wonderland'			4″	Cerise-rose						Free-flowering. Holds color.	
Asparagus Fern	C–W	–	Variable	–	•	•		–	–	Not a true fern but ornamental asparagus. In coastal areas takes full sun. Protect from freezing. Prune off old branches.	Makes permanent mass of green, winters over nicely indoors.
'Meyers'			Upright plumes to 24″ or more	Bright green						Tiny needlelike leaves create fluffy effect.	Useful as focal planting or background.
'Sprenger'			Pendulous, up to 60″	Bright to deep green						Attractive red berries. Variety 'Compacta' small and dense enough for low planter.	Hanging baskets—dependable and graceful.
Aubretia (*Aubrieta deltoidea*)	C	Sp	6″ trailing mat	Blue, red, pink, purple	•	•		20	20	Sow mid-December indoors for bloom in May. Clip off flowers just after bloom to prevent seeding. Hardy.	Hanging baskets, hanging bouquets.
'Monarch Mixture'			6″	Above shades						Widely available mixture.	

Asparagus meyersi

'Glamour' begonia

Name	Warm- or Cool-Season Plant	Season of Bloom	Size and Form	Color	Sun	Partial shade	Full shade	Days to Germination	Sowing to Flowering (Weeks)	Comments	Uses
Bachelor's Button	C–W	Sp, S	10–36″ erect, bushy	Blue, red, pink, white	●	●		10	10	Scorched early by summer heat.	Dwarf forms best for pots. Favored as cut flowers and old-fashioned boutonnieres.
'Jubilee Gem' (AAS)			12″	Deep blue						Neat, bushy habit. Good blue color.	
'Polka Dot' Mix			15″	Blue, red, pink, white						Good habit. Silvery foliage with ruffled flowers.	
'Snowball' (AAS)			12″	White						Heat-resistant. Long bloom period.	
Balsam (*Impatiens balsamina*)	W	S–F	8–30″	Wide range; pink to purple, rose shades, scarlet, white		●		8	12	Takes full sun in cool areas. Camellia and bush types best for containers.	Hanging bouquets; combine with the earliest-to-bloom annuals.
'Color Parade'			10″	Color mix						Large double flowers held well above plants.	
'Tom Thumb'			10″	Color mix						Very compact habit. Profuse bloomer.	
'Double-Flowered Dwarf'			15″	Color mix						Extra-double blooms.	
Basket-of-Gold (*Aurinia saxatilis*)	C–W	Sp	6–12″	Yellow	●	●		14	20	Self-seeds freely. Hardy. Needs fast drainage.	Hanging baskets, hanging bouquets. Beautiful with aubretia.
'Compacta'			6–8″	Bright yellow						Dwarf, compact. Early blooming.	
'Silver Queen'			6–12″	Pale yellow						Like most varieties, has beautiful silvery foliage.	
Begonia, fibrous	C–W	S, F	6–14″ erect, bushy	Red, rose, pink shades, white	●	●	●	14–21	16	Some green-foliage varieties will develop bronze color in full sun. Bright window encourages indoor winter bloom.	Hanging bouquets. Hanging columns. Combine 'Viva' and 'Scarletta' for a red-and-white living bouquet.
'Avalanche' series			6–8″	Pink, white						1″ flowers, tidy plants.	Bred for hanging baskets.
'Cocktail Mix'			6–8″	'Gin', rose; 'Vodka', red; 'Whiskey', white; 'Brandy', pink						Bronze foliage. Compact and sun-resistant.	
'Glamour Hybrids'			8–12″	Red, pink, rose						Large flowers, glossy green foliage.	
'Linda'			6–8″	Deep rose						Free-flowering, compact, weather-resistant.	
'Pizzazz'			8–10″	Mixed colors						Brilliantly colored compact plants.	
'Viva'			6–8″	Pure white						Free-flowering, compact, weather-resistant.	

Browallia

Candytuft, English daisies, and ageratum.

Name	Warm- or Cool-Season Plant	Season of Bloom	Size and Form	Color	Exposure			Days to Germination	Sowing to Flowering (Weeks)	Comments	Uses
					Sun	Partial shade	Full shade				
Begonia, tuberous (*B. × tuberhybrida*)										See "Bulbs in Containers," page 46.	
Browallia	C–W	S, F	8–18″ spreading	Blue shades, white	•			15	12	Blooms profusely. Accepts shade.	Hanging baskets. One of the few brilliant blue flowers. Excellent cut flower. In fall, cut back and pot for winter bloom indoors.
'Blue Bells Improved'			8–10″	Lavender-blue						Base-branching, needs no pinching. Neat and compact habit.	
'Silver Bells'			8–10″	White						Same habit as above.	
'Sky Bells'			8–10″	Powder blue						Good habit. Large flowers.	
Calendula	C–W	Sp, S	6–24″ compact, spreading	Orange, yellow shades, cream	•	•		10	8	Best in cool temperatures. Blooms in winter in mild areas. Earliest color in spring, from fall transplanting.	Plant for late-winter color in pots, boxes, or tubs. Will take sharp frosts.
'Fiesta Gitana' series			12″	Mixture of above shades						Flowers have dark centers.	
'Pacific Beauty'			18″	Mixture of above shades						Heat-resistant. Long-stemmed flowers perfect for cutting.	
Campanula (Bellflower)	C–W	S	4–12″	Blue, purple lavender, lilac, white	–			–		Matting or hanging habit and long bloom make these excellent container subjects.	Hanging baskets, window boxes.
Italian Bellflower (*C. isophylla*)			Hanging, 18–24″	Lavender, blue, white						Vigorous late-summer flowering, dense foliage.	One of best flowers for hanging baskets.
Dalmation Bellflower (*C. portenschlagiana*)			Matting to 4–8″	Bluish purple						Blooms early to midsummer.	Effective as under-planting for shrubs and trees.
Serbian Bellflower (*C. poscharskyana*)			4″ high, trailing to 24″	Lavender-blue						Drought-resistant, summer blooming.	Hanging baskets, edging for large, informal planters.
Candytuft (Annual Iberis)	C–W	Sp, S	6–15″ mounds	Red, pink, lavender, purple shades, white	•	•		8	10	Best in cool-summer areas. Hyacinth flowering type is less hardy, not as good in pots. Sow 2–3 weeks apart for continuous bloom.	Pots, window boxes. Dwarf hybrids best in hanging bouquets. Hyacinth flowering type makes good cut flowers.
'Umbrella Dwarf Fairy'			8″	Many shades of above						Very compact plants. Somewhat heat-resistant.	

Campanula isophylla

Coleus

Name	Warm- or Cool-Season Plant	Season of Bloom	Size and Form	Color	Exposure			Days to Germination	Sowing to Flowering (Weeks)	Comments	Uses
					Sun	Partial shade	Full shade				
Carnation (*Dianthus caryophyllus*)	C	S	12″	Red, white, pink, yellow, pale orange	●			20	24	Double flowers are bright, fragrant, durable. Attractive grayish foliage.	Mass in large container.
'Juliet' (AAS)			10–12″	Scarlet						Fragrant 2½″ flowers.	
'Knight Mixture'			12″	Mixed colors						Large flowers. Stems don't need staking.	
'Mauser's Special' Mixture			12″	Mixed colors						Bred for container culture. Sow seed early.	
Celosia	W	S, F	6–36″ erect	Yellow, gold, purple, pink, red shades	●			10	8	Dwarf varieties best for containers. Many bright-colored varieties available. Cold sensitive.	Plant the plumes in a box next to carrots.
Plumosa Type 'Fairy Fountains'			14″	Color mix						Good base-branching habit. Vigorous grower with long bloom.	
'Fiery Feather'			12″	Red						Uniform pyramid-shaped plumes.	
Cockscomb Type 'Jewel Box'			4–8″	Color mix						Compact miniature plants covered with large combs.	
Coleus	—	W	12–30″ erect	Wide variety of foliage. Color combinations in red, pink, green, and yellow.	●	●		10	—	8–10 weeks from sowing to mature size. Direct filtered light is best indoors. Pinch tips to encourage branching. Many different leaf forms.	Grown for spectacular leaf color. Pot for light shade outdoors, indirect light indoors.
'Carefree'			12″	Available as mix or separate colors						Self-branching. Needs no pinching to maintain excellent habit. Small, closely spaced leaves.	
'Rainbow'			15″	Available as mix or separate colors						More vigorous and larger-leaved than above; needs pinching. Fringed or finely serrated leaves.	
'Saber' series			16″	Mixed colors						Compact habit. Base-branching. "Willowlike" leaves.	Hanging baskets and bouquets.
'Wizard' series			10″	Ten colors						Base-branching, needs no pinching.	

Dahlia

Dianthus

Ivy geranium

Name	Warm- or Cool-Season Plant	Season of Bloom	Size and Form	Color	Exposure			Days to Germination	Sowing to Flowering (Weeks)	Comments	Uses
					Sun	Partial shade	Full shade				
Dahlia	W	S, F	10–12″	Yellow, orange, red, pink, white	•		5	12		From seed or tubers, a brilliant, dependable container plant with a long season. In winter store tubers in cool, dry place, in dry sand.	
'Dahl Face' Mix			10″	Mixed colors						Masses of single flowers.	
'Redskin' Mix			15″	Mixed colors						Large double flowers on compact plants.	
'Rigoletto' Mix			15″	Mixed colors						Early blooming, excellent cut flowers.	
Dianthus	C–W	Sp, S F	3–15″ erect, bushy	White, pink, salmon, red, rose, violet	•	•	7	6–12		Lacy blue-gray foliage. Takes afternoon shade in hot areas. Fragrant flowers.	Dwarf varieties best in pots. Try 'Wee Willie' in an early-season hanging bouquet, combined with strawberries.
'Baby Doll'			8″	Vivid shades of red, pink, violet, white					6–8	Sturdy, compact plant. Plain-edged single flowers.	
'China Doll' (AAS)			10–12″	Pink, red, and salmon shades edged white					10–12	Compact, base-branching. Double flowers in clusters.	
'Indian Carpet' Mix			6″						–	Sow this Sweet William-type dianthus in late spring for bloom the following year.	
'Magic Charms' (AAS)			6″	White, rose, scarlet, pink shades					6–8	Excellent base-branching, compact habit. Fringed, single blossoms, some speckled.	
'Queen of Hearts' (AAS)			15″	Brilliant scarlet-red					12–15	Compact, base-branching; vigorous habit. Single flowers.	
'Wee Willie'			3″ compact mound	Red, rose shades, white					6–8	Long-blooming, sweet-scented, single Sweet William. Very compact. Sow in early spring.	
Fern Squirrel's Foot (*Davallia trichomanoides*)	C–W	–	12″	–		•	•	–	–	Handsome fern forms large mass of ever-green foliage. Take indoors before frost.	Hanging wire basket lined with sphagnum moss, filled with soil.
Gazania 'Sunshine' Mix	W	S, F	8″ erect	Cream, yellow, orange, pink, bronze, and red, some with contrasting zones	•		10	10		Thrives in hot, dry areas. Large, brightly colored 5″, daisylike, long-blooming flowers, many with contrasting centers.	Colorful in large pots and boxes. Blooms until frost.

'Futura' impatiens

'Sprinter Deep Red' zonal geranium

Name	Warm- or Cool-Season Plant	Season of Bloom	Size and Form	Color	Exposure			Days to Germination	Sowing to Flowering (Weeks)	Comments	Uses
					Sun	Partial shade	Full shade				
Geranium, Ivy (*Pelargonium peltatum*)	W–C	S, F	Trailing to 36"	White, red, pink, lavender	●	●		14–21	16	In hot climates, give some afternoon shade. Most plants sold by color, not variety name.	Outstanding hanging-basket plant.
'Mrs. Banks'				White marked with purple						Valued for bicolored flowers.	
'Sybil Holmes'				Pink shades						The most popular basket variety.	
Geranium, Zonal (*Pelargonium hortorum*)	W	S, F	18–24" erect	Red, scarlet, pink, rose, salmon	●			14–21	16	Start seed indoors in February for mid-July bloom. Bring them indoors before frost.	A long-standing favorite for containers indoors and outdoors.
'Carefree'			24" erect with basal branching	Separate colors or mix							
'Red Fountains' hybrid			Base-branching with arching habit	Red	●	●				Combines heat tolerance of zonal geranium with ivy geranium's glossy foliage and some of its trailing tendency.	Hanging baskets, pots. Use 3 plants in 10" basket.
'Sprinter'			18" erect							More dwarfed than 'Carefree', and earlier flowering.	
Impatiens (*Impatiens wallerana*)	W–C	S, F	Mounding, 8–14"	White and many shades of pink, red, orange, mauve; some bicolors		●	●	18	12	Here is the star of the shaded container garden, producing masses of blooms over a long season in deeper shade than most other flowers accept. Pinch to maintain compactness. Varieties abound.	Hanging baskets and bouquets, containers of all types.
'Blitz'			12–14"	Scarlet with bronze leaves						This variety was bred for hanging planters.	
'Duet Mixture'			12–14"	Bicolors						Dwarf plants have double flowers.	
'Futura' series			10–12"	Bright colors						Compact, vigorous growth. Established favorites.	
'Shady Lady' series			12–14"	Bright colors						Unusually profuse bloomers.	
'Sherbet Mixture'			10–12"	Soft pastels						Compact growth, flowers to 2" wide.	
'Super Elfin' series			8–10"	Vivid colors						Especially compact plants.	
'Twinkles' series			10–12"	Fuchsia, red, rose, scarlet						Crisply bicolored flowers on very compact plants.	

'Blue Cascade' lobelia

Marigolds in carpenter's box (see page 90)

Marigolds in vertical planter (see page 93)

Name	Warm- or Cool-Season Plant	Season of Bloom	Size and Form	Color	Exposure			Days to Germination	Sowing to Flowering (Weeks)	Comments	Uses
					Sun	Partial shade	Full shade				
Kenilworth Ivy (*Cymbalaria muralis*)	C–W	Sp, S, F	Trailing to about 24"	Blue	●	●		—	—	This hanging vine, not a true ivy, deserves close inspection for its dainty beauty.	Hanging baskets, or cover beneath shrubs or trees.
Lobelia (*Lobelia erinus*)	C–W	S, F	5–18" trailing or erect	Lavender-blue, pink, white	●	●		18	18	Shearing after first flowering may produce second bloom. Slow from seed. Blooms profusely.	Plant trailing types in hanging baskets at base of shrubs in boxes. Plant erect types in pots and boxes.
'Crystal Palace'			5" erect	Dark blue						Dark bronze-green foliage.	
'Mrs. Clibran' ('Bright Eyes')			5" erect	Violet-blue with white centers						Medium-green foliage.	
'Blue Cascade'			18" trailing	Light blue						Green foliage. Large flowers.	
'Sapphire'			18" trailing	Dark blue with white centers						Light-green foliage.	
'White Lady'			5" erect	White						Effective mixed with colored varieties.	
Marigold	C–W	S, F		Yellow, gold, rust, and orange shades, solids and bicolors	●			7	8–14	Sizes available for every container. Easy care. Profuse bloomer. Many varieties available; following is a sampling.	Dwarf varieties in hanging bouquets. Taller varieties good in tubs or as cut flowers.
'Bolero' (AAS)			12"	Maroon and gold						Double flowers.	
'Happy Face' (AAS)			26"	Deep gold						4" double flowers.	
'Inca' series			14"	Orange, yellow						Compact, early, fully double.	
'Janie' series			8"	Red-gold, gold, yellow						Early-blooming, crested type.	
'Nugget' series			10"	Gold, orange, red, yellow						As early as 6 weeks from seed. Sterile flowers make dead-heading unnecessary.	

Nasturtiums in hanging basket

'Joe Parker' nasturtiums

Nicotiana

Name	Warm- or Cool-Season Plant	Season of Bloom	Size and Form	Color	Exposure			Days to Germination	Sowing to Flowering (Weeks)	Comments	Uses
					Sun	Partial shade	Full shade				
'Primrose Lady' (AAS)			20″	Yellow						Fully double flowers. Staking unnecessary.	
'Red Pygmy'			7″	Mahogany						Very compact double.	
'Naughty Marietta' (AAS)			12″	Gold marked with maroon						Single flowers.	
Moneywort (*Lysimachia nummularia*)	C–W	S	trailing to 24″	Yellow	●	●	●	—	—	Attractive, small, round, waxy leaves and ³⁄₄″ flowers.	Hanging baskets, or cover beneath shrubs or trees.
Nasturtium	C–W	Sp, S, F	12–15″ bushy or 24″ trailing vine	Maroon, red, orange, rose, yellow, cream, solid and bicolor	●			10	6	Best for cool climates. Leaves, seeds, and flowers are edible. Profuse bloomers. Prefer dry soil.	Quick color in pots and hanging baskets. Good cut flowers.
'Dwarf Double Jewel'			12″ bushy	Rose, mahogany, yellow, orange-scarlet						Compact habit. Double flowers held above foliage.	
'Double Gleam' (AAS)			24″ trailing	Complete nasturtium range						Large, sweet-scented flowers, double and semidouble.	
Nemesia	C	Sp, S	8–24″ erect	All colors but green	●			10	12	Lacks heat tolerance. 'Nana Compacta' (10″) dwarf varieties are best for containers.	Charming in hanging bouquets, pots, and window boxes. Pinch to make bushy.
'Carnival Blend'			10″	White, red, orange, yellow						Compact, base-branching plant.	
Nicotiana	W	S, F	8–36″ erect or bushy	Red, rose, lavender, green shades, white	●	●		15	8–10	Prefers afternoon shade in hot areas. Fragrant. Most flowers open in early morning and at dusk.	Excellent in pots. Good for cut flowers.
'White Bedder'			15″ bushy	White						Profuse bloom. Compact, sturdy plants.	
'Dwarf Potpourri' Mix			12″	Mixed colors						Complete color range.	
'Nicki' series			18″	Pink, rose, white						Self-branching and compact. Free-flowering.	

Pansies

'Fanfare' petunia

Name	Warm- or Cool-Season Plant	Season of Bloom	Size and Form	Color	Exposure			Days to Germination	Sowing to Flowering (Weeks)	Comments	Uses
					Sun	Partial shade	Full shade				
Nierembergia	C–W	S, F	6–10" mat	Violet-blue	●	●		15	16	Compact, densely branched, slightly spreading plant. Perennial in mild-winter areas. Profuse bloom.	Pots and hanging baskets.
'Purple Robe'			6"	Violet-blue						Forms dense mat covered with flowers.	
Pansy	C	Sp, S, F	6–8" erect	Full range, some blotched	●	●		10	—	Winter bloom from summer sowing in mild areas. Primarily spring bloom in hot-summer areas. All varieties suited for containers. Smaller-flowered plants sold as "violas."	Hanging bouquets in mixed colors. Many uses in pots, window boxes, and planters.
'Imperial Blue' (AAS)			7"	Light blue with violet face, gold eye						Heat-resistant. Long bloom. Large flowers.	
'Majestic Giant' (AAS)			6"	Wide range, blotched						Large 4" flowers. Blooms through summer.	
Petunia	W	Sp, S, F	12–15" bushy mounds	Wide range, red, pink, blue, purple, yellow, orange, white; single and bicolored	●			12	12–15	Very versatile. All do well in containers. F-1 hybrids are best performers. Choose variety for color and flower form, single or double, ruffled or plain-edged. Many varieties available.	Versatile. All uses: containers, hanging baskets, and hanging bouquets.
Grandiflora varieties										Greatest vigor. Ruffled, large flowers but not as prolific as multifloras.	
Multiflora varieties										More compact and uniform than grandifloras. Best weather resistance. Smaller flowers than above but greater total bloom. Plain-edged flowers.	

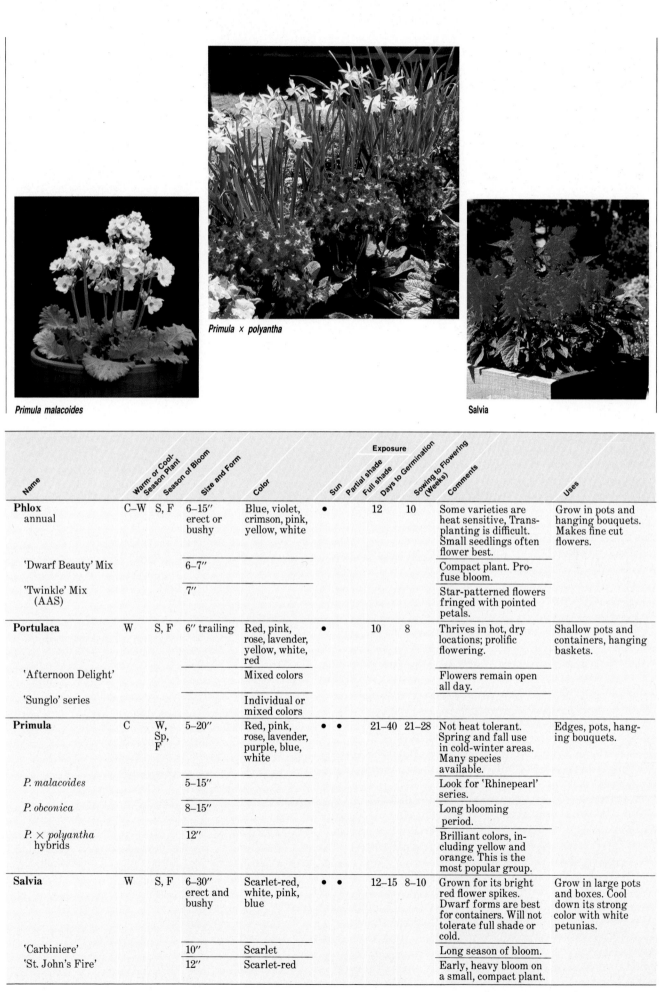

Primula malacoides

Primula × polyantha

Salvia

Name	Warm- or Cool- Season Plant	Season of Bloom	Size and Form	Color	Exposure			Days to Germination	Sowing to Flowering (Weeks)	Comments	Uses
					Sun	Partial shade	Full shade				
Phlox annual	C–W	S, F	6–15″ erect or bushy	Blue, violet, crimson, pink, yellow, white	●			12	10	Some varieties are heat sensitive, Transplanting is difficult. Small seedlings often flower best.	Grow in pots and hanging bouquets. Makes fine cut flowers.
'Dwarf Beauty' Mix			6–7″							Compact plant. Profuse bloom.	
'Twinkle' Mix (AAS)			7″							Star-patterned flowers fringed with pointed petals.	
Portulaca	W	S, F	6″ trailing	Red, pink, rose, lavender, yellow, white, red	●			10	8	Thrives in hot, dry locations; prolific flowering.	Shallow pots and containers, hanging baskets.
'Afternoon Delight'				Mixed colors						Flowers remain open all day.	
'Sunglo' series				Individual or mixed colors							
Primula	C	W, Sp, F	5–20″	Red, pink, rose, lavender, purple, blue, white	●	●		21–40	21–28	Not heat tolerant. Spring and fall use in cold-winter areas. Many species available.	Edges, pots, hanging bouquets.
P. malacoides			5–15″							Look for 'Rhinepearl' series.	
P. obconica			8–15″							Long blooming period.	
P. × polyantha hybrids			12″							Brilliant colors, including yellow and orange. This is the most popular group.	
Salvia	W	S, F	6–30″ erect and bushy	Scarlet-red, white, pink, blue	●	●		12–15	8–10	Grown for its bright red flower spikes. Dwarf forms are best for containers. Will not tolerate full shade or cold.	Grow in large pots and boxes. Cool down its strong color with white petunias.
'Carbiniere'			10″	Scarlet						Long season of bloom.	
'St. John's Fire'			12″	Scarlet-red						Early, heavy bloom on a small, compact plant.	

'Madame Butterfly' snapdragon

Thunbergia alata

Snapdragon bouquet

Name	Warm- or Cool-Season Plant	Season of Bloom	Size and Form	Color	Exposure			Days to Germination	Sowing to Flowering (Weeks)	Comments	Uses
					Sun	Partial shade	Full shade				
Schizanthus	C	S	12–24″	Multicolored flowers (white, pink, yellow, red, purple) vary widely from plant to plant	•			20	14	One of showiest flowers. Plant seeds indoors in March, set out mid-May for late-summer bloom. Variety 'Hit Parade' is compact.	Pots, tubs, hanging baskets and bouquets.
Snapdragon	C–W	Sp, S, F	6–36″	Many red, pink, rose, orange, yellow, bronze, and lavender shades, and white	•			7–14	14	Dwarf forms best in containers. In mild-winter areas, a late-summer sowing produces winter bloom. Cut back spikes after flowering for continuous bloom.	Dwarf types give good show in planters. Tallest varieties make good cut flowers.
'Floral Carpet'			7″	Many of above						Mound-shaped plants produce many 3″ spikes. Long bloom.	
'Little Darling' (AAS)			15″	Many of above						Open flowers (snapless). Compact, base-branching plants with profuse bloom.	
'Madame Butterfly' (AAS)			24–30″	Pink, red, yellow, white						Large, open flowers; heat-tolerant plants.	
Sweet Peas	C–W	Sp, S	8–36″ mounds or climbing vine	White red, pink, blue, and lavender shades, and white	•			15	16	Small bush types best for containers. Profuse, fragrant blooms. Generally heat sensitive. Winter bloom in mild areas.	Grow in large pots and tubs. Good cut flowers. Grow climbers on supports.
'Bijou'			15″ bush type	All of above						Early, heat-resistant plant covered with long-stemmed, ruffled flowers. Needs no support.	
'Galaxy'			Climber	All of above						Vigorous plant blooms from early summer on. Large flowers. Heat-resistant.	
'Knee-Hi Mixture'			30″, will climb	All of above						Compact. Heat-resistant. Large flowers. Needs no support.	
Thunbergia	W	S, F	Trailing to 5′	Orange, yellow, white with black throat	•			12	12–16	Dense foliage. Profuse blooms. Will overwinter in mild areas. Elsewhere makes blooming winter houseplant.	Trailers for hanging baskets, or vine twining up support.
T. alata (Black-eyed Susan vine)				All of above						Flowers 1″ wide.	
T. gibsonii 'Orange Lantern'				Orange with black throat						Flowers 2″ wide.	
'White Wings'				White with chartreuse throat						Flowers 2″ wide.	

Verbena

'Peter Pan' zinnnias,
'Blue Blazer' ageratum

Zinnias

Name	Warm- or Cool-Season Plant	Season of Bloom	Size and Form	Color	Exposure			Days to Germination	Sowing to Flowering (Weeks)	Comments	Uses
					Sun	Partial shade	Full shade				
Verbena	C–W	S, F	4–20″ spreading mounds	Red, pink, blue, purple, and white shades, some with white centers	●			20	10–12	Compact bush type best for containers. Drought tolerant. Profuse bloomer in hot climates.	A native American plant with about the truest red, white, and blue colors available in bedding plants. Vibrant clusters of flowers stand out in pots, window boxes, or hanging baskets. Needs full sun.
'Blaze' (AAS)			8″	Scarlet						Excellent compact habit. Dark green foliage. Large flowers.	
'Amethyst' (AAS)			8″	Blue						Same fine habit as above.	
'Sparkle' Mix			8″	All colors, most with white centers						Same plant form as 'Amethyst' and 'Blaze'.	
'Rainbow' Mix			8″	Mixed, most with white centers						More upright than others. Ideal for pots.	
Vinca (Periwinkle) *Catharanthus roseus*	W	S, F		Red, pink, rose, and white, with contrasting center	●	●		15	12–14		This is the annual vinca, not to be confused with the perennial ground cover (*Vinca major, V. minor*). Bright, phloxlike flowers stand out against glossy foliage. Best in pots and boxes.
Dwarf Type			10″	Same as above						Compact habit; includes 'Little Blanche', 'Little Bright Eye', 'Little Pinkie', and 'Little Delicate'.	
'Polka Dot' (AAS)			6″ trailing	White with red center							
Vinca (Dwarf Periwinkle) (*Vinca minor*)	W–C	Sp	24″ trailing	Blue or white	●	●	●	—	—	Hardiness, handsome evergreen foliage, and pretty blossoms are assets in container garden.	Hanging baskets, or as a cover beneath container shrubs or trees.
Zinnia	W	S, F	6–30″ erect	Wide range of solids and bicolors	●			7	8	Many sizes and flower forms. Best in heat.	Taller varieties can be massed in large containers for showy display and cut flowers. Shorter, bushier varieties are excellent for potted color in full, hot sun.
'Buttons' series (AAS)			10″	Pink, red, yellow shades						Compact habit. Covered with double flowers.	
'Peter Pan' series (AAS)			12″	Orange, gold, scarlet, rose, pink, plum, cream						Compact. Large double flowers are impressive in pots.	
'Ruffles' series (AAS)			24–30″	Cherry pink, scarlet, white, yellow						2½″ ruffled flowers on sturdy plants. Excellent for cutting.	
'Short Stuff' series			8–10″	Coral pink, light pink, orange, red, yellow, white						Flowers like Peter Pan series but plants more compact.	
'Thumbelina' Mix (AAS)			4–6″	Pink, lavender, red, yellow, orange, gold						Starts blooming early, with 2″ double and semidouble flowers.	

*AAS = All American Selection

Bulbs for containers

No group of flowering plants offers brighter, more dazzling color than bulbs. Their flowers are the very essence of the late winter and early spring garden, but there are bulbs as well that brighten the garden in late spring, summer, and fall. Many spring bulbs can be "forced" to bring the freshness of spring indoors in midwinter. Massed in planters bulbs make perhaps the most dramatic display of any group of plants.

Different bulbs require different treatment. Once you know their requirements, you can take full advantage of the opportunities that containers offer for growing and displaying bulbs.

Your choice of bulbs and containers has a lot to do with your success (see the bulb chart on page 46). Ask for planning assistance at your local nursery, or consult bulb catalogs. Bulbs are often divided into spring and fall types, according to when they should be planted, not when they bloom. If you're ordering from a catalog, give yourself plenty of time.

Choose and purchase or order your bulbs as soon as they are available—usually late summer for bulbs to bloom the following spring, or to be forced in winter. If you're not familiar with names and their colors or with the new introductions, ask your nursery attendant for help. Flower colors usually are indicated in the display for each kind and variety.

Plan to use only a single variety in each container; even in the same species, one color may bloom before another, and in the spotlight of a single container the resulting display may be patchy and unattractive. Don't be stingy with bulbs—think in terms of masses of color. If you want many colors grow several containers, each with only one variety, for the most pleasing effect.

By shifting containers that bear blooms of different colors, you can achieve a veritable kaleidoscope of spring. As each container's show of color disappears you can remove it from center stage and replace it with the next colorful performer. Stagger the plantings to extend your flowering spring.

Hyacinths are an exception to the mass-planting rule. Plant one to a

Their dense spikes of blue flowers and intense fragrance make hyacinths an indoor springtime favorite. Planted one to a container, they can easily be moved from room to room.

Daffodils, tulips, hyacinths, and freesias make a dazzling display. *Primula obconica* blooms in the foreground. To last their longest indoors, flowering bulbs in containers need plenty of bright light.

single 4-inch pot instead of putting the bulbs directly into a large container. This extra step lets you see just what you're dealing with: by blooming time, hyacinths vary considerably in height, color, and time of bloom. When they flower, you may want to slip their pots into display planters. After your container-grown spring-flowering bulbs have bloomed, forced or not, don't save them to be grown in the same way again next season. Instead, put them out in the ground to regain the vigor to develop

flowers in future years. Start with new bulbs for your containers next season.

Choosing containers

Your selection of containers will be limited only by the number of bulbs you purchase, the depth of the pot (allow at least 2 inches of potting soil beneath the bulb for good root development), and the need for a drainage hole.

Your containers can be as casual as a coconut shell, or as classic as a clay pot. Bonsai containers lend themselves especially well to bulb display. Bulbs such as *Narcissus minimus*, the tiniest of the trumpet daffodils, are striking in a glazed bonsai container.

Once you've selected your containers and bulbs, you're ready to plant. The following pages outline the procedures.

Planting bulbs in containers

Before you leave the nursery, make sure that each bulb variety is labeled properly. As for soil, a packaged planter mix is easy to use and sterile. Use a light planter mix that won't become compacted. Keep permeability and drainage in mind (see pages 9–10). If you don't want to plant your bulbs right away, remove them from the bag they came in and store them in a cool, dry place.

When you're ready to plant your bulbs, make a tag for each pot showing the variety of bulb. Then take the bulbs out of their bags, one group at a time, and place them shoulder to shoulder in the empty pot, allowing a separation of only ¼ to ½ inch for soil. Follow this procedure with each group of bulbs, being careful not to get them mixed up. Check the bulb chart for the length of time to anticipate before bloom, and the normal flowering period. This is the time to schedule your succession of flowers. With a waterproof pencil or pen on masking tape, label each container with the date planted and stored, and the approximate date to expect blooming. You can remove this tape at flowering time. Put the name tags and bulbs in the labeled containers.

It also pays to keep simple records in a small notebook. Record the necessary data for each container: name of bulb; date entered cold storage; date removed from cold storage; and date of flowering. Also write down any additional information you can think of—it might be helpful the following year. It's surprising how much detail you can forget from one planting season to the next. These records will help you establish a good blooming schedule in succeeding years and point up flaws in your original planning, so that you can repeat your successes and correct your mistakes.

After this "dry-run" planning, you're ready to proceed. *Be sure to concentrate on one container at a time.*

How to plant bulbs in containers

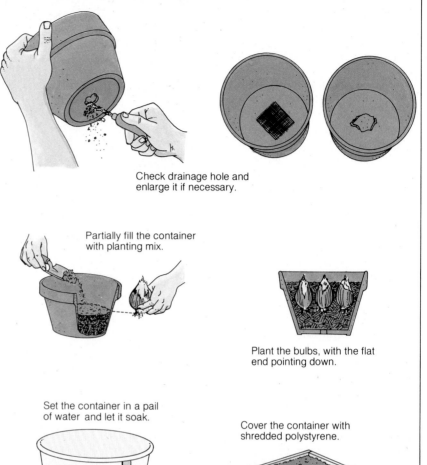

Check drainage hole and enlarge it if necessary.

Partially fill the container with planting mix.

Plant the bulbs, with the flat end pointing down.

Set the container in a pail of water and let it soak.

Cover the container with shredded polystyrene.

Step 1. Check the container to be sure the drainage hole is adequate. If you are using a clay or plastic pot, enlarge the hole with a drill. A hand rasp or "Stickleback" drill is handy for this job.

Step 2. Cover the drainage hole with window screen or curved pieces from a broken pot. This allows the water to drain out, but not the planter mix.

Step 3. Add a bottom layer of planter mix deep enough so that the tops of the bulbs will be 1 inch below the container rim.

Step 4. Plant the flat end—not the pointed end—facing down. If you plant the bulb upside down, it will right itself; but it will take longer, throwing off your schedule and wasting the bulb's energy.

Step 5. Place the bulbs shoulder to shoulder in the pot, firming them in

gently so that they nest in the potting soil, points up. The bulbs should be in the top of the container to allow room for root growth.

Step 6. Once the bulbs are in place, add more planter mix to cover them.

Step 7. Water thoroughly by setting the container in a pail of water and letting it soak until the surface of the soil feels moist. Allow the excess to drain from the bottom of the container. It is now ready for "cold storage." Repeat this for all containers that you want to go into cold treatment right away.

Step 8. Plant the bulbs intended for staggered blooming as described above, but *leave them dry.* Store planted containers in a heavily shaded or dark, dry place at 55° to 65°F. Be sure to mark your calendar—when their time comes, water as above and put them into the cold treatment phase on schedule.

Step 9. Place containers where they can get 12 to 14 weeks of cold treatment at temperatures between 40° and 50°F. Any spot that's cold and dark is satisfactory. An unheated cellar or vegetable storage unit is ideal.

How to store your containers depends on the climate. In moderately cold winters it's all right to store them outdoors by covering them with peat moss or similar material in a trench or box. Shredded polystyrene makes an excellent mulch. It is lightweight, never freezes, and allows water to pass through readily. In severe winter climates, store containers where they won't freeze.

Where winters are too warm to provide a sufficient cold period of 12 to 14 weeks, refrigerate hardy bulbs (especially tulips) for 6 weeks before planting in containers.

The purpose of chilling the bulbs in storage is to give them the environment they need to develop a strong root system to support future shoot and flower production.

During this storage period, roots require moisture for growth. Not only must the soil be moist when the containers are placed in storage, but they must be kept moist (not wet) throughout the storage treatment.

So far, the procedure for growing bulbs for display in containers *outdoors* is the same as for "forcing" bulbs for early bloom *indoors*. At this point, however, the procedures differ. For indoor display, force early bloom as described below. For outdoor display, do nothing. Let the flowering come naturally.

Step 10. Now the forcing. At the end of the 12 to 14 weeks, when the sprouts are 2 to 5 inches high and the roots can be seen at the drainage hole, place the containers in a cool (60°F) room. After a week or two, they are ready for normal room temperature. Be sure to give them adequate light at this point or the growth will be leggy.

After bloom, keep the leaves growing as long as you can. If you plan to put the bulbs out in the garden when true spring arrives, put them in a cool place (50° to 55°F). Never remove the leaves until they are brown and papery. Food manufactured in the leaves is stored in the bulb for next season's growth.

With staggered planting, daffodil bulbs can be moved in sequence into a bright, cool room to provide blooms for several weeks. Foliage can be tied or braided to keep it from sprawling until it dries out.

These golden daffodils were forced indoors in a sunny location.

Left: 'Paper White' narcissus is among the easiest bulbs to force. Above: Amaryllis (*Hippeastrum*) can be forced year after year if it is properly fed, sunned, and rested.

Forcing hardy bulbs

It's easy to force tulips, daffodils, ornithogalum, hyacinths, and the "little" bulbs—crocuses, snowdrops, and grape hyacinths—to bloom indoors ahead of their normal outdoor time. Grow them as Christmas gifts, for friends. Read the catalogs carefully, and select the largest bulbs obtainable. It doesn't pay to buy anything but the best when you use bulbs for forcing. Choose those the firm recommends for forcing, or buy the ones listed on this page and page 44. If you order by September, the bulbs will be delivered in early fall. Then follow these instructions:

Soil mixture. The soil mixture for bulbs should be made of equal parts of soil, sand, and peat moss. To each 5-inch pot of this mix, add a teaspoon of bone meal. If you don't want to bother mixing soil, buy a soilless medium. However, this is costly for large quantities. (For instructions on mixing your own soilless medium, see page 11.

Pot size. The kind and quantity of bulbs you plant determine what size container to use. One large daffodil or tulip bulb can be planted in a 4- or 5-inch diameter pot in which three crocuses or other smaller bulbs would

fit. For six tulips, daffodils, or hyacinths, you'll need a 6- to 10-inch pot. Cover the tops of tulips and hyacinths with ½ inch of soil. With daffodils, don't try to cover their necks—just the fat portion of the bulb. Cover smaller bulbs like crocuses with ½ inch of soil. Then water thoroughly. You can also purchase preplanted containers of bulbs that are conditioned to begin the forcing process.

Temperature. Bulbs need a cool period after potting so they can form a vigorous root system. Without a potful of roots, they cannot bloom prolifically later on. Years ago, the usual practice was to bury these pots of bulbs in a bed of cinders outdoors in a coldframe, leaving them there until at least New Year's day. This system is impractical for most of us today, however; besides, there are easier ways to accomplish the same thing. Find a cool, dry, frost-free place where bulbs can be forced. An unheated garage attached to the house, a cool attic, or a cool basement will do. A temperature range of 35° to 55°F will promote good root growth. Keep the soil evenly moist throughout this period.

When to start forcing bulbs. You can begin forcing bulbs when the leaves begin to push upward—usually some-

time after January 1. To have blooms over a longer period, bring a few pots indoors each week to a sunny, cool (55° to 70°F) place. The cooler the air, the longer the flowers will last. Keep bulbs away from sources of heat such as radiators and gas heaters. Keep the soil moist at all times. Bring all pots to be forced into warmth and light by late February.

Narcissus to force. These fragrant-flowered relatives of the daffodil are delightful subjects for forcing in a semisunny to sunny location. The bulbs are available in autumn. Plant them in moist pebbles in a bowl, or pot them in a mixture of equal parts of soil, sand, and peat moss, kept moist. Either way, place the bases of the bulbs 1 to 1½ inches deep in the growing medium. Water thoroughly, drain, and set in a cool (50° to 65°F), dark place for the roots to form. After the bulbs have a good root system (which usually takes two to four weeks), put them in a warm, bright, sunny spot. There they will bloom quickly, in fragrant clusters of white or gold.

After forcing 'Paper white' or 'Paper yellow' (cultivars of *Narcissus tazetta*), discard the bulbs if you live where winter cold dips below 20°F. In the other areas, plant them in the garden outdoors. Don't try to force them again. Buy new stock each year.

Daffodils to force. 'King Alfred' and 'Golden Harvest' are big, classic, golden daffodils that force perfectly. 'President Lebrun' has pale yellow petals and a dark golden cup. Short-cup varieties good for forcing are 'John Evelyn' and 'Scarlet Leader'. Miniatures such as 'W. P. Milner', 'March Sunshine', and *Narcissus obvallaris* (Lent Lily), force beautifully and take up little space.

Tulips to force. 'Brilliant Star', 'Ibis', 'Prince of Austria', 'Rising Sun', 'Murillo', 'Scarlet Cardinal', 'Willemsoord', 'Scarlet Admiral', 'Bartigon', 'Niphetos', 'Rose Copland', William Pitt', 'Gudoshnik', 'Golden Harvest', and 'Fantasy'.

Hyacinths to force. 'Jan Bos', 'L'Innocence', 'Bismark', 'Gertrude', 'Lady Derby', 'La Victoire', 'Grand Maitre', 'Ostara', 'Perle Brilliante', 'City of Haarlem', 'Queen of Pinks', and 'King of Blues'.

Forcing hyacinths in water. You can grow hyacinth bulbs in water in specially designed containers or jars, or any type of vase that will hold the bulb in the top and allow the roots to reach into the bottom section. Fill the vase so the base of the bulb just touches the water. A small piece of charcoal in the container will keep the water sweet and retard the development of harmful bacteria. Place it in a dark, cool area until the roots are developed before you move it into the light. Change the water weekly. Flowers and foliage develop rapidly. Use any of the varieties listed previously in this section.

"Little" bulbs to force. Little bulbs such as crocuses, snowdrops, and grape hyacinths (*Muscari*) are sometimes forced, but their lifespan is so brief indoors that it is really a shame to waste time on them, especially since they last days or even weeks longer when planted naturally outdoors.

Other bulbs to force. In addition to the standbys, consider calla lily (*Zantedeschia*), amaryllis (*Hippeastrum*), Cape lily (*Veltheimia viridifolia*), freesia, iris (*I. reticulata* and the Dutch, English, and Spanish types), Easter lily (*Lilium longiflorum*), shamrock (*Oxalis*), and squills (*Scilla siberica*).

Problems in forcing bulbs. Don't expect many problems with the bulbs you force, but you may have a few. Tulips

Anemones and fuller-flowered ranunculus (in the foreground).

Ranunculus (foreground) and pansies.

almost always have some aphids, either on the leaves when they emerge from the soil or on the flower buds. Spray them carefully with a houseplant insecticide. Flower buds of forced bulbs will blast (fail to open) if the soil is allowed to dry out severely after they've begun to grow. Sometimes bulbs have basal rot; this condition is seldom your fault. If the foliage suddenly stops growing and turns yellow, give it a gentle tug. Chances are you'll find it loose in the pot, and a rootless, rotted bulb in the soil. Discard the soil and rotted plant material—don't put them in the compost pile. Disinfect pots by soaking them for ten minutes in a solution of one part household bleach to ten parts water. Be sure to rinse pots thoroughly.

After the flowers fade. At this time, keep the foliage in good health by providing moisture and sunlight. As

soon as the danger of hard freezing is past outdoors, move the bulbs to a sunny, out-of-the-way place where the foliage can continue to mature and store up strength for another year's blooms. Although the bulbs cannot be forced again next year, you will find them a good addition to the outdoor garden. Plant them when you bring them out of the house, or leave them in the pots until the following autumn, transferring them then to the open ground.

A note about ranunculus and anemone bulbs

You can grow these bulbs successfully in containers, but don't force them. Unlike most bulbs, they need no special storage temperature or air circulation—just a rest once their blooming period is over. However, they must be stored dry or they may rot. It's not easy to fool them about

For a concentration of color, crocus bulbs have been planted closer together than they would be if they were planted in the ground.

Nothing else brightens a shaded spot so effectively as green-veined white or light pastel caladiums.

the seasons. They're tender to frost, but you can give them an early start indoors by providing good light; just don't keep them cold and moist and dark in storage. Anemone and ranunculus bulbs are worth planting— spring is not complete without a few tubs of these colorful flowers to brighten the container garden.

A note about miniatures

There's no need to restrict miniature flowering bulbs to rock gardens; they are also delightful in pots.

To keep such dainty miniatures as *Iris danfordiae* from getting lost in a border or bed, bring them closer to the eye. Check the bulb catalogs for the miniatures of crocus, iris, daffodils, and other bulbs. Whenever rock garden bulbs are discussed, visualize the flowers in a pot or bowl display.

It's easy to transfer bulbs from a rock garden to a container garden.

Here's how Reginald Farrer describes rock garden crocus in his classic work, *The English Rock Garden:*

"*Crocus imperati* is one of the very loveliest, emitting, first, its prostrate dark leaves, and then, wrapped in twin spathes, a chalice of blossom, opaque creamy buff outside, and feathered richly with lines of dark purple. . . .

"*Crocus ancyrensis* (Golden Bunch) opens in February, a little golden star rarely touched with brown, and with scarlet stigmata.

"*Crocus susianus* (Cloth of Gold, [now called *C. angustifolius*]) has cups of brilliant orange gold, heavily striped with dark brown varnish outside, and opening into a wide star with so much heartiness that the segments often go too far and turn down the other way. It opens with the first warmth of the February sun and is a native of southern Russia.

"*Crocus chrysanthus* can be told from all other golden crocus by the black spot on the barb of the anthers. The species is most variable but invariably beautiful, the type being of pure stainless yellow, but the forms diverge on to sulphur-yellow and differing shades of blue, with diversities of blue feathering."

A note about caladiums

In mild-winter areas, treat yourself to the showy foliage of the caladium. This member of the arum family is a tuberous-rooted perennial from tropical South America. Its "flowers" are interesting but insignificant— caladiums are grown purely for their spectacular leaf colors. Try as many colors as you can locate at your local nursery, or order from specialty growers' catalogs—they include silver, white, pink, red, bronze, and green in a variety of combinations.

Store the bulbs dry in vermiculite or peat moss after the foliage dies back. Then, around January, bring them out for potting and reviving for the spring show. They enjoy a night temperature that is constant at not less than 60°F; keep the potting mix evenly damp. Plant three tubers to an 8-inch pot, allowing plenty of depth for root development. Use any good planter mix. When the first leaves peek through the soil, increase their light from subdued to north window bright. Keep the humidity about 60 percent. They'll come along much faster if you use a heating cable beneath the pot. If you don't have a heating cable, you can use a light bulb beneath an upturned pot, as shown.

As the weather warms outdoors on a shady patio, gradually get the plants used to the outdoor location with other shade plants. Their lovely foliage adds color and textural contrast when placed among ferns and *Chamaedorea* palms. Caladiums should have frequent but very light feeding, such as a light dilution of fish emulsion, and evenly dry soil. Be sure to maintain adequate drainage. Caladiums are also very good house plants if you can provide sufficient humidity.

To keep the soil evenly warm . . .

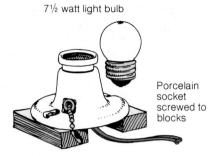

7½ watt light bulb

Porcelain socket screwed to blocks

Put the light under an upturned pot with the planted pot on top to keep the soil evenly warm.

A note about pests

Pests usually ignore bulbs planted in containers, but they will take an occasional nibble from the flowering parts. The most common culprits are snails and slugs, and occasionally earwigs. Thrips rarely invade the container garden, especially if you're using artificial soils. Snails and slugs are about the easiest garden pests to control in a container garden if you stay one step ahead of them.

The foliage of bulbs is usually unappetizing to the regular pests. If a problem does appear, it's easy to remedy as you would with other plants in containers (page 17).

Bulbs for containers

Name	Height	Planting Depth	Sun	Partial shade	Full shade	Planting Season	Flowering Season	Comments
Allium (Flowering Onion)	9–60″	2–4″ depending on size	●			Fall	Depends on species: spring–summer	Many species in a wide range of colors. Long bloom season. Small species like *A. neapolitanum* are ideal for containers.
Agapanthus	18–48″	Just below surface	●	●		Spring or fall	Midsummer	Leave in same container year after year. Divide only infrequently—every 5–6 years. Evergreen dwarf forms 'Dwarf White' and 'Peter Pan' (blue) are fine when potted.
Anemone	6–24″	1–2″	●	●		See text	Late winter–early spring	See text. Red, pink, blue, rose, or white flowers.
Begonia, tuberous	12–20″	Just covered–½″		●	●	Winter	Summer–fall	Flowers in many shades of red, pink, yellow, orange, or white. Becomes leggy in dense shade. Best in filtered shade, cool temperature, high humidity.
Caladium	9–30″	Just covered		●	●	Spring	– –	See text. Red, pink, green, and white foliage colors. With proper storage, can be left in the same container.
Canna, dwarf	18–30″	5–6″	●			Midspring	Late summer–early fall	Large flowers in many colors. Attractive, tropical-looking green or bronze foliage. With proper frost-free storage, it can be left in same container. Remove faded flowers after bloom. After blooming, cut stalk at soil level.
Clivia	12–36″	Top just above soil		●	●	Fall	Early spring	Yellow, orange, or red flowers. Use as indoor plant in cold-climate areas. If kept moist, it can be left in the same container.
Crinum	24–36″	Neck exposed	●			Spring or fall	Spring–summer	Flowers in shades of white or pink, often striped red. Best left undisturbed in container moved into frost-free place.

Tuberous begonias

Marigolds, dahlias, and coleus.

Name	Height	Planting Depth	Sun	Partial shade	Full shade	Planting Season	Flowering Season	Comments
Crocus	4–5″	Just covered	●	●		Fall	Depends on species; generally, late winter–early spring	See text for variety description. Flowers in shades of blue, purple, gold, and white. In warm areas, refrigerate for 4 weeks before planting. Withhold water in summer.
Dahlia	12–48″	6″	●	●		Spring or fall	Summer	Many flower forms and colors; dwarf varieties best for containers.
Freesia	10–18″	2″ deep	●			Fall	Late winter–early spring	Flowers white, pink, red, lavender, purple, blue, yellow, and orange. Fragrant. May need staking. Tender in cold climates. Grow indoors until frost is past.
Hippeastrum (Amaryllis)	24–36″	Half covered	●	●		Available late October	Indoors, begins 4–6 weeks after planting	Best indoors or frostproof outdoor area. Flowers large, in shades of red, pink, and white.
Hyacinthus (Hyacinth)	6–12″	5″	●			Fall	Early spring	Refrigerate bulbs for 6 weeks in warm-winter areas. Many soft pastel shades. Dutch types are fragrant. Bulb size relates directly to size of flower spike.
Iris, Dutch	10–24″	Covered 1″	●	●		Midfall	Early spring in mild areas–late spring in cold	Flowers in blue, purple, yellow, orange, and white shades. Plant 5 to a 6″ pot. Good for forcing.
Ixia	18–24″	Covered 2″	●			Fall	Late spring	Flowers in red, pink, yellow, orange, and white with dark centers. Tender. See Freesia.
Lilium (Lily)	18–60″	5–6″	●	●		Late fall or early spring	Spring-summer (depends on variety)	Many flower forms and colors. Plant bulbs as soon as you get them. Require constant moisture but excellent drainage. One bulb to a 6″ pot; several to larger container.
Narcissus (Daffodil)	5–20″	Covered 2½ times width of bulb	●	●		Early fall	Spring	Plant early and late varieties for extended blooming season. Many single and bicolor shades of red, orange, yellow, and white. 'Angel Tears' and 'Hoop Petticoat' are perfect dwarf varieties for small containers.
Ornithogalum (Star of Bethlehem)	10–14″	4–5″	●	●		Early fall	Midspring	White flowers with contrasting green stripe on each petal (*O. umbellatum*).
Ranunculus	10–24″	Covered 1″	●			Winter	Late spring–early summer	See text; flowers in shades of red, pink, yellow, orange, and white. Best in cool climates.
Tigridia	18–30″	2–4″	●	●		Early spring	Mid to late summer	Large flowers in red, pink, yellow, and white shades with dark speckles.
Tulipa (Tulip)	5–30″	2½ times width of bulb –4″ to 6″	●	●		October. As late as December in frost-free areas	Spring–depends on variety	Many flower colors and varieties. Don't ignore species tulips like *Tulipa kaufmanniana* (Waterlily Tulip)–they are ideal in pots. Require 4–5 week cold period. In warm-winter areas, refrigerate for 4 weeks before planting.

Trees and Shrubs in Containers

From Abelia through Wisteria, there's a tree, shrub, or woody vine for every purpose and location in the container garden. Select dwarf or slow-growing varieties, keep them well pruned, and enjoy them for years.

Growing trees and shrubs in containers is an ancient practice. Commercial nursery traders brought frankincense trees in containers from the Somali coast to Egypt about 3,500 years ago. And even before then— about 4,000 years ago—Egyptians grew trees in large "boxes" or "pots" cut into rock and filled with planting soil.

Today you can walk through nurseries and find almost countless plants that thrive in containers. In fact, *all* plants can be grown in containers, at least in the early stages of growth. When you select trees and shrubs for container culture, it makes sense to choose dwarf or slow-growing types, which will accept container conditions for years. The dwarfing effect of containers, along with occasional pruning, will keep even the most vigorous shrubs and trees within bounds for a long time.

Listed below are some of the best shrubs and trees for container culture.

◀

This pine bonsai is several years old, but you can create a beautiful instant bonsai by carefully pruning and shaping a Japanese black pine.

Included in the shrub list are a few outstanding woody vines. As you read through the descriptions that follow, keep these points in mind. On a spring morning, caught up in the excitement of choosing and planting those big stars of your container garden, the shrubs and trees, you might overlook two crucial facts: (1) Big containers are heavy, and the trees and shrubs they hold are unwieldy and difficult to transplant. So choose ample, sturdy containers. (2) Even though a shrub or tree is hardy enough to survive local temperatures, it might freeze in a container. So be prepared to protect roots, or entire plants if necessary. See page 16.

Shrubs for container culture

Abelia × grandiflora (Glossy Abelia). Evergreen to semideciduous. Offering a colorful combination of foliage and flowers, this shrub has coppery new leaves that gradually turn glossy green, as well as gracefully arching branches. Flower clusters bloom white to pinkish white from early summer into fall. Prune selectively in late winter. For best color, grow it in full sun. Hardy to 0°F.

Abelia grandflora

Berberis thunbergii 'Atropurpurea' (Purple-leaf Japanese Barberry). Deciduous. The finely textured, colorful foliage of this shrub makes it a good portable barrier. Leaves are bronzy red in spring and summer, and yellow, orange, and red in fall. Red berries are revealed after the leaves drop. It has a dense habit and arching, heavily thorned branches. It can be sheared, but is more attractive when pruned selectively. Grow it in full sun. Hardy to −20°F.

Variety 'A. Nana' is dwarf.

Bougainvillea hybrids (Bougainvillea). Evergreen. Some forms of this woody subtropical vine are suitable for container culture. They are often grown with great success as hanging-planter subjects. Among them are 'Raspberry Ice' with bright red flowers and variegated leaves, and 'Crimson Jewel' with crimson flowers. Transplant them with great care, as the roots are fussy. Hang them in a sunny, sheltered southern exposure. Take them indoors during winter except in frost-free areas. Hardy to 35°F.

Buxus microphylla koreana (Korean Boxwood). Deciduous. Although well-known as a small hedge or edging plant, this boxwood is most picturesque when trained into a formal shape and planted in a container. It stays low-growing (3 feet) and compact without severe pruning, and has bright green leaves. It grows well in sun or partial shade, and is hardy to −15°F.

B.m. japonica and its several varieties and *B. sempervirens*, including the dwarf variety 'Suffruticosa', are excellent container shrubs.

Camellia hybrids (Camellia). Evergreen. All members of this handsome genus grow well in tubs if they are given acid soil, partial shade, and protection from drying winds. Each variety blooms sometime from fall to late spring. In very cold areas, a cool sunporch is ideal for them in winter. Some small, sprawling varieties of *Camellia sasanqua* (*C. hiemalis*) lend themselves beautifully to hanging planters. Among the best are 'Showa-No-Sakae' and 'Shishi Gashira'. Give them shelter from heavy rain. Hardy to 25°F.

Chaenomeles species and hybrids (Flowering Quince). Deciduous. For the earliest spring excitement, the flowering quince deserves center stage among the shrubs. It is one of the earliest spring bloomers, and its

Bougainvillea

flowers come in shades of white, red, and pink. Leafless branches and flowers have an appealing oriental look. Leaves are tinged red when young, then gradually turn lustrous green. This shrub is easily pruned to shape or espalier and requires little care. Hardy in all areas.

Chamaecyparis obtusa (Hinoki False Cypress). Evergreen. Slow to outgrow its place and easy to keep below 6 feet, this tree can be trained to reveal its attractive irregular branching pattern. The Dwarf Hinoki Cypress (*C. obtusa* 'Nana'), growing only 3 feet high, is round-headed with deep green foliage on layered branches. The Golden Hinoki Cypress (*C. obtusa* 'Aurea') has golden new foliage that gradually turns deep green. All Hinoki False Cypress make excellent bonsai specimens. They are unsatisfactory in hot-summer areas, and are hardy to 10°F.

Cleyera japonica (Cleyera). Evergreen. This slow-growing shrub (6 to 8 feet) has colorful foliage on gracefully arching branches. New brownish red leaves gradually turn a lustrous deep green, retaining a red midrib. Small

clusters of fragrant white flowers bloom in spring, followed by dark-red berries lasting into winter. Grow as you would its relative, the camellia. Hardy to 0°F.

Cotoneaster species (Cotoneaster). Within the genus *Cotoneaster*, two species adapt well to growing in baskets: creeping cotoneaster (*C. adpressus*) and bearberry cotoneaster (*C. dammeri*). Creeping cotoneaster is a deciduous shrub that grows slowly to a height of 12 inches and bears pink flowers followed by bright red berries. Bearberry cotoneaster also provides a cascading display of white flowers and red berries. It has evergreen foliage and reaches a height of 6 inches. Grow cotoneaster in full sun or partial shade. Hardy in all areas.

Cycas revoluta (Sago Palm). Evergreen. One of the most striking plants for containers, this relic of distant geologic ages has characteristics of both fern and palm. Very slow growing, it seldom exceeds 2 or 3 feet in height, even in old age. It prefers little water and fertilizer. Take it indoors in winter. Hardy to 20°F.

Buxus microphylla

Camellia sasanqua

Elaeagnus pungens (Silverberry). Evergreen. The gray-green foliage of this shrub adds a silvery sparkle wherever it's used, and the small silver-white flowers are fragrant. Brownish flecks on leaves and stems reflect the sunlight. On its own it grows as a low, sprawling shrub, but is easy to keep neat by pruning. It is a tough container plant, good for wind and sun protection. It is available in variegated leaf and dwarf forms. Hardy to 15°F.

Euonymus fortunei radicans (Wintercreeper). Many varieties of this woody evergreen vine make hardy ground covers, and their wide-spreading habit works for hanging baskets as well. Keep wayward branches pruned when grown in hanging baskets. The purple-leafed wintercreeper variety 'Colorata' will drape nicely, as will the green and white variegated form 'Gracilis'. Grow in full sun or partial shade. Euonymus is hardy in all areas.

Fuchsia × hybrida (Fuchsia). Deciduous or evergreen. Selected varieties of fuchsias are at the top of the list for hanging-basket plants in the "fuchsia climates"—the cool coastal areas. In hot-summer regions, fuchsia enthusiasts must resort to mist spraying to give the plant the climate it needs. Fuchsias will survive a light frost, although leaves and young growth will be injured. In hard-frost areas treat as an annual, take cuttings for next spring, or bring the entire plant indoors. Spring is the time for pruning. Cut back approximately the same amount of growth made the previous summer, or remove frost-injured wood. Fuchsias bloom early and continue through summer to frost. Hang baskets in a location protected from wind and in a partially shaded exposure. In cold-winter areas fuchsias can be overwintered by cutting them back and packing their containers in plastic trashcans of moist sawdust or vermiculite, stored at about 40° to 50°F. Hardy to 32°F.

Hedera helix varieties (English Ivy). Evergreen. In addition to the regular garden form of this classic woody-stemmed ground and wall cover, with its 2- to 4-inch leaves, there are many attractive forms of miniature variety 'Baltica'—all perfect for hanging baskets. Some have variegated or

Fuchsia trained as a standard

Hydrangea macrophylla

Juniperus procumbens 'Nana'

ruffled leaves. In addition to their beauty and ease of cultivation is the advantage of their year-round uniform appearance. If you can't find them at the nursery, try houseplant stores and florists. Some favorites are 'Hahn's', 'Fluffy Ruffles', 'Gold Dust', 'Needlepoint', 'Pixie', and 'Silver King'. Hardy in all areas.

Hibiscus rosa-sinensis (Chinese Hibiscus). Evergreen. Yielding lavish summer color, this plant sports glossy leaves and large (4 to 8 inches), showy, single or double flowers in shades of pink, red, yellow, and white. Choose among many varieties for flower color and plant habit. Warm weather and sun will promote the best bloom; it needs afternoon shade in hottest areas. Since it is cold sensitive (hardy to 20°F with overhead protection), bring it indoors in cold-winter areas.

Hibiscus syriacus (Althea). Deciduous. This widely used member of the Hibiscus family blooms in an array of single or double flowers (2½ to 3 inches) in summer. Foliage is bright green, unevenly toothed, and sometimes lobed. Erect and compact when young, it requires more pruning to shape when older. In winter, partially prune last year's growth for larger flowers the following summer. It does well in partial shade or fall

sun and is hardy in all areas.

Hydrangea macrophylla (Hydrangea). Deciduous. This shrub creates a soft feeling that seems to invite relaxation. Large clusters of white, pink, red, or blue flowers hide the foliage in summer and fall. Flower color is easily manipulated by soil pH, turning blue in acid soil and deepest red in alkaline. Large leaves (8 inches) are glossy and toothed. It has an even, round habit. Prune to desired size. Grow it in full sun in cool-summer areas, in afternoon shade in hot-summer areas. Hardy to −10°F.

Ilex species (Holly). Evergreen. The glossy green foliage and bright red berries are a classic reminder of the holiday season. For large, long-lasting berries on a slow-growing compact plant, try Chinese holly (*Ilex cornuta* 'Burfordii Nana'). Hardy to 0°F. The many forms of English holly (*I. aquifolium*) are just as good in containers, although less tolerant of dry heat. Dwarf forms of yaupon holly (*I. vomitoria*) with small spineless leaves make excellent container shrubs. All are hardy to 10°F.

Juniperus species (Juniper). Evergreen. These handsome patio companions come in enough forms to fit any garden need. The slow growth of *Juniperus chinensis* 'San Jose' makes

it a top container shrub. Semiprostrate and very compact, it has sage-green foliage. It does well trained into formal shapes, or as a bonsai specimen. The Hollywood juniper (*J. chinensis* 'Torulosa') is an erect shrub (to 10 feet) with artistically twisted branches that are easy to train. The Blue Pfitzer (*J. chinensis* 'Pfitzeriana Glauca') has silver-blue foliage on arching stems (to 10 feet), and can be trained into many shapes.

Several of the spreading types will spill and drape in hanging baskets. Shore juniper (*J. conferta*) is a natural trailer, adapted to seashore conditions, but it also has good heat tolerance in interior conditions. Bar Harbor juniper (*J. horizontalis* 'Bar Harbor') is fast growing and will spread 10 feet in the open. The grayish blue foliage turns plum colored in cold weather. Andorra juniper (*J. horizontalis* 'Plumosa') is a wide-spreading juniper with a flat-branching habit and gray-green foliage that turns plum in winter. Blue Carpet juniper (*J. horizontalis* 'Wiltonii') is a very low-growing juniper with striking silver-blue color. *J. procumbans* 'Nana' has graceful, heavy branches with irregular growth and stubby, dense, blue-green foliage. All are hardy in all areas.

Lagerstroemia indica (Crape Myrtle). Usually thought of as a tree (see page 56), crape myrtle is also grown as a small hanging-basket shrub. The 'Dixie' series makes cascading 24-inch mounds and includes ten different flower colors. 'Bayou Marie' is a dazzling bicolor. 'Bourbon Street' is watermelon red. Hardy to 15°F.

Lantana species (Lantana). Evergreen or deciduous. In mild-winter areas this trailing shrub can add year-round color to the container garden. Plants are easily damaged by light frosts, but usually they survive to give a full bloom the following year—just trim out dead wood to maintain a neat appearance. Put in a warm, full-sun spot, and don't over water or over fertilize. Take indoors in cold-winter areas. Some of the more colorful cultivars are 'Gold Mound' (yellow-orange), 'Confetti' (pink, yellow, and purple), and 'Carnival' (crimson, lavender, yellow, and pink). Trailing forms make excellent hanging basket plants. Particularly good is the 'Spreader' series. Hardy to 25°F.

Lavandula angustifolia (English lavender). Evergreen. Highly valued for its fragrance, this small (12- to 48-inch) shrub is a pleasant addition to any patio. Strongly fragrant lavender to purple flowers are borne on long (18- to 24-inch) spikes in mid-summer. Its gray foliage is aromatic. Prune after flowering to maintain compactness. Hardy in all areas. Other species of lavender and varieties of English lavender are occasionally available.

Mahonia aquifolium (Oregon Grape). Evergreen. Good for year-round color. Leaves are divided into many spiny leaflets resembling holly leaves. Bronzy red new growth gradually turns dark green, then purplish or bronze in winter cold and full sun. Yellow flower clusters in spring are followed by long-lasting dark purple edible fruit. Control shape and size by pruning. The plant is hardy to −20°F, with protection.

Nandina domestica (Heavenly Bamboo). Evergreen. A light, airy shrub with an oriental, bamboolike feel, it has many slender, unbranched stems bearing softly textured leaves divided into leaflets. Pinkish bronze foliage gradually turns green, then picks up a purple or bronze tinge in fall, and becomes scarlet in the winter sun. Although it grows to 6 to 8 feet, it is easily controlled. Dwarf varieties

Rhododendron

are available. Heavenly bamboo produces bright red berries in fall on the female plants if one male plant is nearby. Hardy to 5°F.

Pinus mugo (Mugho Pine). Dwarf forms of this pine, often labeled 'Compacta', 'Gnome', or 'Slavinii', remain tiny, compact shrubs. With a little pruning, a specimen makes a striking bonsai. Mugho pine is an ideal candidate for container growth. If you find that yours is getting higher than you want it, pinch new, soft green shoots (candles) to 1 inch in spring. Foliage is attractively dense. Hardy in all areas.

Potentilla fruticosa (Bush cinquefoil). Deciduous. A carefree container plant, this shrub withstands heat, drought, poor soil, and cold temperatures. Yellow to orange flowers bloom from late spring to early fall. Grayish green to green foliage has divided leaflets. It grows low (1 to 4 feet), with a mounding habit. 'Klondike' is one cultivar that stands out as a prolific bloomer with a compact habit. Hardy in all areas.

Rhododendron species and hybrids (Rhododendron and Azalea). Some deciduous, most evergreen. These numerous, magnificent plants adapt beautifully to container culture, as long as they have ample containers, acid soil, generous water, fast drainage, protection from burning sun in hot climates, and protection from extreme cold. Small types of rhododendrons are easiest for container culture. All evergreen azaleas adapt. For hanging baskets, *Azalea macrantha* 'Gumpo' (white) and 'Gumpo Pink', both spreading and slightly pendulous, are excellent choices for spring color. Like citrus, the more tender azaleas and rhododendrons need indoor protection in winter, although a few deciduous azaleas are hardy to below 0°F if their containers are insulated.

Spiraea species (Spiraea). Deciduous. The long bloom and dwarf, compact habit (2 to 3 feet) of *Spiraea bumalda* 'Anthony Waterer' justify its use on the patio. It bears flat-topped clusters of rosy pink flowers from late spring to fall. The fountain-shaped *S.* × *vanhouttei* also deserves attention; its blue-green leaves grow on gracefully arching branches, and it sports showy white flowers. Flowers are borne on new growth, so the plants benefit from heavy pruning. Prune in summer for spring bloomers, late winter or early spring for summer-flowering varieties. Hardy to −20°F.

Acer Palmatum

Trees for container culture

If your favorite tree is missing from this list, remember that the list is by no means exhaustive. It is limited to trees that in most cases do not require a great deal of effort to keep them pruned and shaped for container display.

Acer ginnala (Amur Maple). Deciduous. In fall this is one of the most brilliantly colored maples. Whether it is trained as a single- or multiple-trunked tree, its bright scarlet leaves will brighten up your patio in autumn. Don't keep the Amur maple hidden until fall, though; its small, fragrant spring flowers are followed by red-winged fruits highlighting the beautiful dense green foliage. Hardy in all areas.

Acer palmatum (Japanese Maple). Deciduous. The Japanese maple in its various forms is commonly used in cool-summer Northwest gardens. It grows so slowly that it can be held in a tub for years as a small, dainty containerized tree. Many grafted garden forms are smaller than the seedlings. Of these, you might consider:

'Burgundy Lace'. Soft lacy effect. Deeply cut, serrated burgundy leaves on green stems.

'Dissectum'. Easily trained. Low, weeping habit. Finely cut, fernlike green leaves are scarlet in fall.

Most cultivars are hardy to −20°F.

Callistemon species (Bottlebrush). Evergreen. Bottlebrush makes a good summer companion for any patio. Its bright red flowers resemble stiff bottle scrubbers. It blooms from late spring to summer, but may flower occasionally throughout the year. These subtropical trees will tolerate only a light frost. Try these varieties:

Lemon Bottlebrush (*C. citrinus*).

Erect. Hardy to 30°F. Profuse bloom. Leaves are 3 inches long. Young foliage has a coppery tinge.

Weeping Bottlebrush (*C. viminalis*). Drooping branches. Leaves are 6 inches long. May need support and pruning. 'McCaskilli' is a well-behaved cultivar. Hardy to 30°F.

Cercis canadensis (Eastern Redbud). Deciduous. For an early spring flower show, the redbud will satisfy even the most demanding observer. Small, pealike clusters of pink, purple, or white flowers completely cover the leafless branches. Heart-shaped leaves provide summer shade ideal for patios, and turn yellow in fall. Showy seed pods are revealed in late fall after the leaves drop; they remain on the tree into winter. Of the many cultivars, 'Forest Pansy' is of interest, with pinkish purple flowers and foliage on red stems. 'Alba' is a profusely flowering variety. Hardy to −20°F.

Callistemon citrinus

Cornus florida

Ginkgo biloba

Chamaedorea elegans (Parlor Palm). This evergreen has typical fish-skeleton-like leaf bases sheathing the single trunk, merging in a cluster at the top.

Several other palms lend themselves equally well to container culture.

The paradise palm (*Howea forsterana*) has similar leaves on a clean, interestingly scarred, 9-foot stem.

The pygmy date palm (*Phoenix roebelenii*) grows slowly to 6 feet. Its airy leaves emerge from the top of the slender stem.

The lady palm (*Raphis excelsa*), an old favorite in containers, grows 6 to 12 feet tall. Its many stalks bear oriental-fan-like foliage at the tips, making for a bushy, bamboolike effect.

These palms are strictly tropical plants, and won't take freezing. But some others will. For example, the popular Mediterranean fan palm (*Chamaerops humilis*) withstands temperatures in the teens or lower, if the container is insulated.

Cornus florida (Flowering Dogwood). Deciduous. The flowering dogwood signals the beginning of spring with a spectacular show, and it deserves to be featured in your landscape. Flowers appear before foliage, in shades of red, pink, rose, or white. Foliage turns bright red in fall, highlighted by red berries. Its slow growth when young (to 10 or 15 feet) makes it a good container candidate. It is a perfect companion for the eastern redbud (*Cercis canadensis*). Hardy to −20°F.

Crataegus phaenopyrum (Washington Thorn). Deciduous. Put this tree in a container on your patio and you'll be rewarded with color through spring, summer, and fall. White flowers bloom profusely in spring to early summer. Attractive clusters of red berries appear in late summer through winter. Lobed leaves are brilliant orange-red in fall. It has a dense, graceful, low-branching habit. Hardy to −20°F.

Eriobotrya japonica (Loquat). Evergreen. For a close-up tropical effect, this tree certainly deserves attention. Large (12 inch) leaves are heavily veined, deeply toothed, dark green on top, and fuzzy brownish red beneath. It is less than showy, but the extremely fragrant white flowers will fill your garden with a spicy scent in fall. It bears attractive yellow edible fruits in winter. Selective pruning will hold it to container size (10 to 12 feet) for years. Cut branches are good for arrangements. This subtropical fruit tree is hardy to 0°F but will bear fruit only in warmer climates.

Ginkgo biloba (Ginkgo). Deciduous. This large tree can be held to container size for years. Its light green, fan-shaped leaves dance in the wind, providing a summer-long attraction whether moving or still. In the fall the leaves turn a rich, bright yellow. The fact that this prehistoric species survivor is sometimes called the oldest tree on earth hints at its hardiness and versatility. Give it the toughest spot in the garden and watch it thrive. To be sure you get a male tree (fruits of the females are messy and have an unpleasant smell), choose named cultivars such as 'Autumn Gold', 'Lakeview', or 'Sentry'. Hardy to −20°F.

Gleditsia triacanthos 'Inermis' (Sunburst Honey Locust). Deciduous. This tree makes up for its lack of flower color with golden-yellow new foliage highlighted by the older, light green leaves. The overall effect is of a wonderful yellow canopy from spring to fall. Softly textured leaves are finely divided into small leaflets. The entire tree turns yellowish gold in fall. Ideal for close quarters and containers. Hardy everywhere.

Lagerstroemia indica (Crape Myrtle). Deciduous. In summer, when flowering trees are hard to find, the crape myrtle comes across in style. Crinkled, crepelike flowers in shades of white, pink, rose, or lavender bloom over a long period. The light green leaves turn orange-red in fall. The mottled tan bark and branching pattern are more apparent during the leafless winter months and add a note of interest to a possibly bland landscape. The root system is sufficiently cold-hardy to encourage cold-winter use. A group of crape myrtles called Indian Tribe has superior hardiness, performance, and mildew resistance. Named cultivars include red-flowering 'Cherokee', purple-flowering 'Catawba', pink-flowering 'Potomac' and 'Seminole', and light lavender 'Powhatan'. The tree is generally hardy to 0°F, but check the tolerance of individual cultivars.

Ligustrum lucidum (Glossy Privet). Evergreen. An admirable performer in large tubs, the glossy privet will reach tree size quickly and thrive in tight quarters for years. Large feathery clusters of white flowers appear in spring, followed by dark blue fruit in quantity. The foliage is luxurious, rich green, and glossy. Easily trained into many shapes, single- or multiple-trunked. Hardy to 20°F.

Magnolia grandiflora (Southern Magnolia). Evergreen. The spring elegance of the magnolia makes it one

Lagerstroemia indica

of the most attractive trees to grow in a container. Large (up to 10 inches across) fragrant flowers bloom in spring to early summer in shades of white, pink, and purple. Colorful, interesting seed capsules follow the flowers. Leaves are giant (up to 12 inches long by 5 inches wide), stiff, and glossy green.

Magnolias outgrow their containers eventually, but smaller, slow-growing forms of southern magnolia, like 'St. Mary', are handsome in boxes for years. Even though it is a southern native, magnolia is usually hardy to 0°F.

Malus species (Flowering Crab Apple). Deciduous. Considering the many varieties of crab apple available, there's surely one to fit your garden scheme. Valued for their delicate, profuse spring flowers in shades of white, pink, and red, the crab apples come in a wide range of habits and foliage colors as well. The tree shape ranges from weeping to columnar. Leaf color is primarily green, but some leaves retain a reddish bronze color for the entire season. Fruits are attractive from fall to early winter. When selecting a variety of crab

apple, be sure to watch for disease resistance and hardiness of individual cultivars. These crab apples suitable for containers have acceptable disease resistance:

Japanese Flowering Crab Apple (*M. floribunda*). Moundlike and horizontally branching. Flowers are pink, fading to white. Fruits are yellow-red, 3/8 inch.

Parkman Crab Apple (*M. halliana* 'Parkmanii'). Gracefully arching purple branches. Flowers are large, double, rose. Fruits are dull red, 1/4 inch.

Cultivar 'Red Silver'. Irregularly branched, yet graceful. Reddish or purple-bronze foliage. Flowers are deep wine red. Fruits are purplish, 3/4 inch.

Sargent Crab Apple (*M. sargentii*). Lowest and broadest of the crab apples (8 to 10 feet high and 12 feet wide). Flowers are white. Fruits are small, red, in clusters.

Nyssa sylvatica (Sour Gum). Deciduous. The drooping branches of this picturesque tree bear lustrous, dark green leaves that form a very dense head of great ornamental value. In fall the leaves turn a dazzling scarlet orange.

Picea glauca 'Conica'

Wisteria

This tree is certain to be the focal point of any garden. It bears inconspicuous flowers in spring, followed by dark blue fruits in summer (usually hidden by foliage). Hardy everywhere.

Picea glauca 'Conica' (Dwarf Alberta Spruce). Evergreen. You can probably look over the top of even an old specimen of this dwarf conifer, which grows only about an inch a year. Fine-textured, dense, and perfectly conical, it is a favorite as a living Christmas tree. (If you take it indoors for Christmas, give it light, keep it away from dry heat, and return it to its outdoor spot in 10 days or sooner.) Protect from unusually hot sun and drying winds. Hose it down occasionally in hot weather. Hardy in all areas.

Pinus thunbergiana (Japanese Black Pine). Evergreen. A favorite for bonsai training, it is equally valuable as a tub specimen. It grows slowly, and may take three to four years to reach 4 feet. In a large container, given time, it will become a small tree, though easily shaped and kept at desired size. Hardy in all areas.

Podocarpus macrophyllus (Yew Pine). Evergreen. This slow-growing tree (not a true pine) is valuable indoors and out. Leaves are 4 inches long and narrow. The yellowish green new foliage contrasts nicely with the older, dark green leaves, giving a fernlike effect. Good in containers. A tender native of Japan, it is hardy to 10°F.

Prunus species (Flowering Plums). When you think about the flowering plums, you have to consider more than the spring flowers alone; their purple foliage is a strong element in any garden.

Prunus cerasifera 'Atropurpurea' and its related forms – 'Thundercloud', 'Newportii', 'Vesuvius' – are widely available.

P. × blireiana is a popular fruitless tree. It has reddish bronze foliage and bears pink double flowers, in contrast to the pink single clusters of the 'Atropurpurea' forms. *P. blireiana* also has a lighter, more graceful form than the 'Atropurpurea' and its variations. Hardy in all areas.

Prunus caroliniana (Carolina Cherry Laurel). Evergreen. No bright, unusual colors here – just a dense, glossy tree that offers a luxurious touch of green. Small white flowers bloom in late winter or early spring, with black berries following. Whether single- or multiple-trunked, it is easily trained into formal shapes. Two cultivars ideal for containers are 'Bright-n-Tight' and 'Compacta'. Hardy to 0°F.

Pyrus kawakamii (Evergreen Pear). Evergreen. Left untouched, it becomes a sprawling shrub. Tied to a trellis or wire, it can easily be trained as an espalier. Staked, it makes a handsome single-trunked tree. The glossy green foliage is a year-round attraction. Fragrant white flowers are abundant in late winter or early spring. It is fast growing. Heavy pruning reduces flowering. Hardy to 20°F, it may not survive extreme cold.

Wisteria species (Wisteria). Deciduous. This vigorous woody vine can be trained as a small, single-trunked tree with an umbrellalike top. The "tree" produces the same long, lovely clusters of blossoms that have earned this long-lived woody plant the description "queen of the vines." Flowers are borne in spring in shades of white, pink, blue, or lavender. Their fragrance is evocative of warm spring evenings. Leaves are 12 to 18 inches long and are divided into leaflets. Hardy to −20°F.

Fruits and Vegetables in Containers

In this chapter you'll find information about dozens of varieties of fruits and vegetables that you can grow even in the most limited space. Citrus and deciduous dwarf fruit trees, prolific strawberries, and new varieties of vegetables make it easy to grow your own food.

Although many compact varieties of fruit have been developed recently for container culture, growing fruit in containers is nothing new. One of the most famous container-fruit gardens belonged to Louis XIV, who in the 1600s constructed an orangerie at Versailles. The orangerie was the predecessor of the modern greenhouse, and tender trees could be grown in it to produce fruit out of season. Some of the fruit trees at Versailles are said to have lasted 75 years. Of course, you don't need to think or work on such a grand scale as Versailles, and for wherever you live there are dwarf fruit trees that don't require a greenhouse.

The development of modern dwarfing techniques has considerably reduced the work required—dwarf trees are far less likely to get rootbound or to have problems with watering and feeding. Dwarf trees, both grafted and genetic, are discussed in detail

◀

'Marsh' seedless grapefruit is handsome even between flowering and coloring of fruit. Tucked beneath is a Transvaal daisy.

later in this chapter; but first, here are some step-by-step planting and maintenance techniques that will keep your portable orchard healthy and productive for years.

Climate and container-grown fruit trees

As the Versailles garden shows, planting in containers allows even tender plants far from their natural climate zone to grow well; you can move them to shelter when cold weather comes, and wheel them to a shady spot when it gets too hot. Containers allow you to try lemons in Michigan and peaches in North Dakota, as long as you have a winter holding site that is neither too cold nor (for citrus) too dry. Deciduous fruit trees demand no light when dormant and will withstand considerably lower temperatures than citrus. Be careful not to overwater while the plants are inactive. Citrus is decorative enough to be brought into the house and put in front of a south window. You can put deciduous trees like cherry and apple in the garage or in a basement cold enough to satisfy their chilling requirements. They will probably survive the winter

there very nicely—but get them out into the sun on fine spring days.

Remember, just because a plant can survive winter in the ground doesn't mean that it can manage cold weather in a container. If your garden soil freezes, then container soil definitely will freeze and your plants will die. Plants in containers do not have the protective insulation of the soil that plants in the ground do. If you live in the coldest northern zones, protect even hardy deciduous plants in the coldest months if they are left outdoors (see page 16).

Choosing plants

Our variety lists and the section on dwarf trees will give you more extensive information on fruit suited to container culture. For now, here are just a few deciduous types: Apples on Malling 7, 9, or 26 dwarfing rootstocks, and of course genetic (true) dwarf apples; pears grafted onto quince roots; genetic dwarf peaches, nectarines, apricots, and cherries; all figs; the smaller-tree crab apples; genetic dwarf citrus; and spur-pruned grape varieties. Several fruit trees are available grafted onto newer dwarfing rootstocks such as Citation. Some

Citrus (foreground) and deciduous fruit trees in temporary fiber containers at a nursery.

combinations are available on a single grafted tree—for example, several apple varieties, or peach-nectarine-apricot, or other combinations. Besides tree fruits, there are many strawberry varieties suitable for containers.

Choosing containers

Begin your orchard with containers that are just 2 or 3 inches wider than the roots of your plants. If you start with a bare-root apple or pear or a genetic dwarf fruit, your first container should be about the size of a 5-gallon can. In fact, since it will only be in use for one growing season, you might actually use a lard or nursery can, covered with a basket or box to disguise it. Let the young tree grow for a season and fill the container with roots; then repot it the following spring.

Evergreen fruit plants such as citrus should start out in a container that's not too much bigger than their rootball. If your soil mix is well drained, you can go to a box 3 or 4 inches wider than the roots all around. With large nursery plants, the first container may be the last.

Permanent containers should be no larger than necessary so they won't be unwieldy, although you might consider a platform on wheels for any large container. A half barrel is about the right maximum size; so is any box or pot that holds about that volume of soil. Permanent containers should be no smaller than about 18 inches on a side and 18 inches deep. The smaller

the container, the more work is involved in feeding, watering, and root pruning.

A container that can be taken apart is most practical. You can attach one side with screws; better yet, you can screw all four sides together for easy removal. Container trees must be removed from their pots every two or three years for root pruning (see the sketches on page 14). Otherwise all the feeder roots will bunch at the walls of the containers and the plants will languish.

Move plants from the first (5-gallon size) container to the bushel size over two or three seasons. When a plant has the appropriate size container, it can find water and nutrients easily. The right size also keeps soil from going sour around and beneath the roots, and slows top growth.

Choosing the right soil mix

To a commercial or homemade planting mix of sand and organic material, some gardeners like to add a little rich loam. It holds water better and helps keep nutrients available. Add up to one third loam if you like, but be careful not to include clay soil. It holds water too well for a container mix, and you may drown your plants. With a purely synthetic mix (see discussion of synthetic soil, page 9), be careful about feeding; the nutrients you add leach away when you water. Keep to a regular schedule, as outlined below.

Fertilizing

Let the growth of the plant and its general appearance determine your feeding schedule. A deciduous plant should leaf out and grow vigorously in the spring and early summer, and the leaves should be a healthy medium green. Yellow leaves suggest a lack of nitrogen; very dark leaves may mean you're feeding too much.

One method of feeding is to give each plant about half the recommended quantity of complete fertilizer (containing nitrogen, phosphoric acid, and potassium or potash) every two or three weeks rather than the full amount once a month. A liquid fertilizer is easy to handle and less likely to burn roots. If the directions say 1 tablespoon per gallon of water, use half the amount (1½ teaspoons) instead, and fertilize twice as often.

You can also use one of the pellet slow-release fertilizers. These dis-

solve slowly over a period of time, so they won't wash away with the first watering.

Feed throughout the growing season if the plant is to receive winter protection. Stop about mid-July if it is to stay outdoors. That will give it a chance to harden up new growth.

Citrus requires about the same amount of feeding as deciduous fruit, but it may also require a few extra nutrients. Special citrus foods containing iron, zinc, and sometimes other minerals are available at nurseries. Use them regularly, or switch to them if you see leaves with yellowed portions between bright green veins. If the leaf is uniformly yellow, veins and all, the plant lacks nitrogen. Citrus food can also be used on deciduous plants without harming them, but it may cost more than deciduous plant food.

A note of caution: When drainage is poor, fertilizer can build up in a pot and burn the plant. If you see brown, dry-looking leaf edges, water heavily as described in the following section on watering. This heavy watering (leaching) will clean the soil.

Watering

Your container-grown plants should never be allowed to wilt, but neither should they stand in soggy soil. If you check the soil occasionally by digging down an inch or two, you'll soon learn how much to water. The top inch may stay moist for a week in fairly cool weather; however, when the weather is hot and windy, water frequently—perhaps even every day for a plant that needs repotting. Frequent watering is why well-drained soil is so important—you can pour on the water without drowning the roots.

Mulch will help keep the soil moist and cool. Use a coarse organic mulch such as bark chips, and pile it about 2 inches thick. In really hot weather, group your containers to help conserve moisture and provide partial shade.

Don't count on rain to do all your watering, since plants in containers may act as umbrellas and shed most of the rain. Check the soil even when rainfall has been abundant. Rain will enable you to water less often, however—the moist air will keep water from evaporating.

To keep harmful mineral salts in water and fertilizer from building up in the soil, always water thoroughly, filling the pots until the water runs freely from the drain holes. After you have watered the last pot, go back and fill the pots a second time.

If you live in a hard-water area, where water leaves bathtub rings and doesn't produce good lather, not only should you water thoroughly, you should also leach the soil in each container every month or so. Leaching is a long soaking that dissolves any accumulated mineral salts and flushes them away. Let your garden hose run in each container for about 20 minutes, slowly enough that the container doesn't overflow at the top. Failure to water thoroughly and to leach occasionally will inevitably result in brown leaf edges, then dead leaves, and finally dead plants.

When you leave home, group your containers near a water source out of the afternoon sun. The grouping will help keep them moist; the shade will cut the need for water; and if they're near a hose none will be overlooked by your vacation waterer. For large numbers of containers, you can buy a water timer that will turn the water on at regular intervals. Just hook up a system of small hoses that run permanently to each container. A commercial drip system is effective here too, provided you filter the water before it goes into the system. Filtering is necessary because the drip openings are small and easily clogged. Filters are available at most garden centers.

Potting and repotting

There are many successful potting methods, and gardeners have great success with methods you'll never see recommended in books (except this one). These suggestions should work every time and keep your plants healthy.

The ideal container soil holds water but never gets soggy. Water should soak in immediately, not sit on top, and should run out just as fast. Choose a synthetic soil or a mixture of synthetic soil and garden loam. Moisten the soil until it's barely damp but not wet. Sprinkle and stir the soil one day to make sure that it's evenly moist, then pot your plants the next day.

Be sure your pot or box has good drainage holes. If you buy a container with one small hole, drill two or three more, or ask the nursery attendant to

The acid fruits of calamondin can be used like lemons or limes, or to make marmalade.

do it for you. If you plan to use a can for a season, punch a dozen holes around the bottom with a beer can opener. Cover the holes with broken pieces of pot or broken crockery. The soil mix should fill the pot from top to bottom.

Place enough soil mix in the pot, lightly tamped down, so that the roots touch it when the crown of the plant is just below the pot rim. Hold your bare-root plant at that level and add enough soil to support it, tamping lightly as you go. Then finish filling to about $1/4$ inch below the pot rim. The soil will settle, leaving you room to water. For an evergreen plant, or any plant in a nursery container, simply place it on the first layer of soil, then fill around it. Before covering the rootball, scratch it all around with a fork to roughen up the roots and get them pointing outward. Cut off any long, spiraling roots at the bottom of the rootball.

To repot, use a similar technique as described in the illustrations. Repotting is necessary because plants tend to bunch their feeder roots at the wall of the container, where they dry out faster. Even when cared for properly, a potted plant will eventually need more water and nutrients than it can get in a pot that is too small for it. Shave off an inch of root and add fresh soil to allow the plant

to grow healthy young roots and to give the empty soil around them a reservoir of moisture. Always clip the top back a little when you shave off the roots to balance the plant. New top growth will follow the new root growth.

After potting and repotting, soak the soil thoroughly.

Growing citrus fruits

Growing your own citrus fruit will certainly seem worthwhile when you breakfast on homegrown oranges, but the dwarf trees described here do have conditions to be met. They need direct sun at least half of every bright winter day; comfortable room temperatures; and moist, humusy soil (equal parts of garden loam, peat moss, and sand). Feed with a liquid houseplant food every 2 to 4 weeks, and give the plants a shower with tepid water once a month. Keep them outdoors during frost-free weather.

Invest only in dwarf varieties developed specifically for pot culture. These will produce fragrant flowers all year, as well as edible fruit. If leaf yellowing occurs, correct it by using a fertilizer formulated especially for acid-loving plants.

To produce fruit indoors, you may need to emulate the bee and do some pollinating. With an artist's brush, transfer pollen from the stamen of one flower to the stigma (the pistil end protruding beyond the petals) of another.

Here are a few varieties of dwarf citrus that are well adapted to containers.

Calamondin (*Citrofortunella mitis*). This dwarf citrus will produce abundant 1- to 2-inch, orangelike fruits every month of the year. Leave them on the tree to brighten your surroundings, or use them to make marmalade.

Otaheite Orange (*Citrus* × *limonia*). This miniature version of the sweet orange produces 1- to 2-inch fruits, which taste more like a lime than an orange. They will remain on the tree for as long as two years.

'Improved Meyer' Lemon (*Citrus limon* 'Meyer'). This dwarf tree is a relatively old variety, bearing flowers that range in color from lavender to white, followed by bright yellow lemons with thin skin and sweet flavor.

'Ponderosa' Lemon (*Citrus limon* 'Ponderosa'). Probably the most spectacular of the dwarf citruses, this one has glossy green leaves, sharp spines, and lemons that weigh from 1 to 3 pounds. Each one takes about six months to mature, but this plant will have fruit at varying stages of maturity, year-round. When fruits reach maturity, you will need to prop the branches with stakes.

Persian Lime (*Citrus autrantiifolia* 'Tahiti'). For full-sized fruit, this is the dwarf lime to grow. The fruit is bright chartreuse-green, and the plant is easily kept under two feet high.

Dwarf 'Washington' Navel Orange (*Citrus sinensis* 'Washington' Navel). This popular juice orange bears in areas too cool for successful cultivation of other oranges. Harvest from winter into spring. Fruit peels easily. Maximum height of tree is 8 feet.

Other dwarf citruses available are grapefruit, limequat, tangelo, citron, tangerine, and Nagami kumquat.

Growing dwarf deciduous fruits

On page 59 we mentioned growing certain deciduous fruits in containers, including those grafted onto dwarfing rootstocks. The most compact and altogether most satisfactory container growers, however, are the genetic (true) dwarf varieties developed especially for container culture. Full-size fruit is borne heavily—sometimes so heavily that developing fruit requires thinning. Most trees grow

Espaliered apple tree

slowly to no more than 5 to 8 feet. Many of these varieties have been developed by Floyd Zaiger of Modesto, California, and are marketed by retail nurseries all over the country. Here are some of the dwarfs.

'Garden Delicious' Apple. Derived from the popular 'Golden Delicious', this fruit can be eaten fresh or used for cooking. To encourage early growth, remove all fruit the first year before it develops, and most fruit the second year. It is self-fertile. Remove suckers from rootstock. This is the most widely available dwarf apple.

'Garden Annie' Apricot. This semi-freestone takes three years to reach harvesting size. Among the larger genetic dwarf trees, it needs occasional pruning to keep its center open to air and light. Self-fertile.

'Garden Bing' Cherry. Slow-growing to about 6 feet, it has a 4-foot spread. Occasional branches revert to standard size and should be removed. Self-fertile.

'North Star Sour' Cherry. This tangy cooking cherry bears large fruit in late June on a tree that reaches 8 feet. Self-fertile.

Among the latest developments are these "Babes":

'Honey Babe' Peach. Only 4 to 6 feet tall at maturity, its stems are especially close-noded, so it bears heavily. Freestone fruit is early ripening, and quality is excellent. It is exceptionally beautiful in bloom and in fruit. Prune to keep center open. Self-fertile.

'Nectar Babe' Nectarine. Comparable in fruit quality, and in beauty of blooms and fruit, to 'Honey Babe'

peach, it bears prolifically. It also needs occasional pruning to keep its center open. It is self-fertile but bears more heavily if there is a 'Honey Babe' peach close by.

Growing some unusual fruits

Besides the more common container fruits already discussed, you may want to grow some of the following fruits as well. All are easy, and most are widely available.

Dwarf Pomegranate (*Punica granatum* 'Nana'). Delicate red flowers grow on branches of pale green leaves in summer. Tiny edible fruits appear in autumn. Another variety (*P. granatum* 'Chico') does not bear fruit, but has 1-inch orange flowers.

Edible Fig (*Ficus carica*). Varieties

Pomegranate

Strawberries in tub

Strawberries in planter

produce green, yellow, or purplish fruit. This is among the easiest deciduous fruit trees to grow. Plant in a large tub with ordinary garden soil, give it sun, and keep it moist during the growing season. In cold climates, the trees will need complete winter protection. Dwarf forms are available, making seasonal mobility easier.

Natal Plum 'Fancy' (*Carissa grandiflora*). This hybrid bears white, starlike flowers and red, cranberry-flavored fruit that can be used to make a fine jelly.

Pineapple Guava (*Feijoa sellowiana*). This small evergreen tree or shrub bears spectacular 1- to 2-inch red flowers and edible green fruit. Root it from cuttings during warm weather (it needs high humidity) in sand or perlite. Then grow in loamy soil with plenty of sand and humus.

South American Tree Tomato (*Cyphomandra betacea*). Delicious, egg-shaped, red fruit is sweeter than ordinary tomatoes and excellent for making jam.

Growing strawberries

You can grow strawberries in hanging baskets, in clay and wooden strawberry barrels, in 5-gallon plastic pails, in planter boxes, and along walls.

For maximum production, the container should be large enough to nourish a root system that's at least 8 inches wide and 8 inches deep. Restricting the root system in a con-

tainer that's too small reduces production; reducing any part of the root system affects the entire plant.

Instead of planting eight crowns, try planting only four plants to a 48-inch-long planter box. You will probably get more berries over a longer time. The soil should be fairly rich with organic matter and should drain well. Don't set the plants too high in the soil, or the top part of the roots will dry out. Similarly, don't set the crown of the plant below the surface of the soil or it will rot.

If you're using a disease-free soil mix, you don't have to worry about verticillium wilt and red stele (root rot), since both are caused by soil-borne fungi. It's best to start with plants certified to be virus-free. In general, these will out-produce other varieties and will bear good crops for three years or more.

The performance of strawberries from year to year is not exactly predictable. The quality of the same variety may differ from one year to the next due to differences in weather and soil conditions. Also, the "best" variety in one location may be only fair in another. Varieties available at local garden centers are adapted to your area, and you can also check with the office of your County Agricultural Extension Agent for suggested varieties.

Recommended standard varieties. 'Cyclone'. Early. Large, delicious

berries are good for freezing. Plant is winter-hardy and resistant to foliage diseases.

'Jerseybelle'. Late. Firm berries are good for freezing. This variety is very productive for a late strawberry.

'Surecrop'. Early. This large, round, glossy, firm variety is of good dessert quality. Space large plants 6 to 9 inches apart for top production. Resistant to red stele, verticillium wilt, leaf spots, leaf scorch, and drought.

'Tioga'. Early. Productive plant bears large, firm, sweet berries. It is unusually successful in mild-winter and hot-summer areas where most strawberries do poorly.

Recommended everbearing varieties. 'Fort Laramie'. Produces large, firm, flavorful berries over a long season. Hardy.

'Ogallala'. Medium-sized berries are dark red, soft, and tasty. Good for freezing. Vigorous grower. Hardy.

'Ozark Beauty'. Large, sweet, tasty berries are bright red outside and inside. Production occurs on mother plants, but not on runner plants during summer and fall.

'Quinalt'. Large, exceptionally sweet berries are produced sometimes even on unrooted runners. Good for freezing. Vigorous grower.

'Sweetheart'. Very sweet, medium-sized berries are produced about 120 days after this variety is planted from seed. This is the only full-size strawberry grown from seed.

Vegetables for containers

When you start growing vegetables in containers, you are joining a vast and expanding group of enthusiasts. Economy, recreation, ornamental value, and expanding the variety of available vegetables are advantages of container gardening. Maybe you used to have a vegetable garden but now live in an apartment or condominium with only a balcony, patio, or roof area for gardening, yet you don't want to give up growing your own vegetables. Whatever your motives, you have no doubt discovered the superior flavor of a vine-ripened tomato or tender, sweet, home-grown corn.

When you grow vegetables in containers, you can take advantage of the various microclimates around the house and garden. For example, you might plant the heat-loving egg-plant in a spot where it gets not only full sunlight but also the reflected heat off a south wall.

You can use all sizes of pots, cans, plastic buckets, plastic trash containers, garbage cans, bulb pots, azalea pots, fiber pots, paint buckets, half barrels, and fruit baskets (peck and bushel). The larger the container, the more soil you'll need. A large amount of soil allows the plant roots to draw on a reserve of moisture and nutrients. It is easier to water and feed plants in large containers than in small containers, since the latter require more frequent care. However, suit your container to the plant; it doesn't make sense to give a plant a soil depth of 16 or 18 inches if it can produce in a container 6 to 8 inches deep.

When gardening on a balcony or roof, you must consider the weight of the containers for the sake of safety. To get 50 square feet of planting space with 16-inch-deep containers, you need 67 cubic feet of soil mix. If the containers or boxes are 8 inches deep, you need only half that amount of soil.

Choosing and using containers for vegetables

You must find containers that are the right size for your special needs. There is no such thing as a standard-size container except for old clay pots, which are uniformly graduated from 2 to 16 inches. A gallon-size container is described by different manufacturers as $7^{1}/4'' \times 6^{1}/4''$, $7^{1}/2'' \times 7^{1}/2''$, and $6^{1}/4'' \times 7''$. The dimensions indicate diameter and depth. The thickness of the material—fiber, metal, type of plastic—and the taper of the pot account for the differences in dimensions.

Sizes of typical containers in inches and gallons:

1 gallon—$7^{1}/4'' \times 6^{1}/4''$	4 gallon—$12'' \times 11''$
2 gallon—$8'' \times 8''$	5 gallon—$12'' \times 12''$
3 gallon—$10'' \times 10''$	6 gallon—$13'' \times 13''$

A vegetable garden in containers

The containers in this garden would take up less than 75 square feet of patio, deck, or balcony space. We positioned the containers on a 6′ × 20′ balcony as shown below.

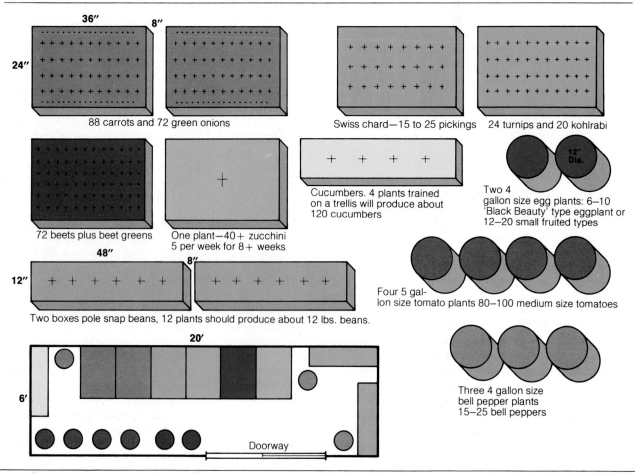

88 carrots and 72 green onions

Swiss chard—15 to 25 pickings

24 turnips and 20 kohlrabi

72 beets plus beet greens

One plant—40+ zucchini 5 per week for 8+ weeks

Cucumbers. 4 plants trained on a trellis will produce about 120 cucumbers

Two 4 gallon size egg plants: 6–10 'Black Beauty' type eggplant or 12–20 small fruited types

Two boxes pole snap beans, 12 plants should produce about 12 lbs. beans.

Four 5 gallon size tomato plants 80–100 medium size tomatoes

Three 4 gallon size bell pepper plants 15–25 bell peppers

Doorway

Vegetables in containers

The dedicated urban gardener can always find a space to grow fruits and vegetables.

Sizes of standard redwood octagonal planter tubs:

12″ × 11″	16″ × 14″
14″ × 12½″	18″ × 15″

With a substantial vegetable harvest as the goal, the following plan for a patio or balcony garden has been worked out to show the kind of container-crop yield possible. After a year of experimenting, test gardeners settled on three types of containers:

For onions, carrots, beets, turnips, kohlrabi, and zucchini, they used 24″ × 36″ boxes, 8 inches deep.

For pole beans, cucumbers, and peas, they used a narrow 12″ × 48″ box, 8 inches deep. Many also built a trellis for training these vegetables to grow vertically.

For peppers, eggplant, and tomatoes, they preferred the single 4- and 5-gallon containers.

Typical plantings in a 24″ × 36″ box might include four rows of carrots, 5 inches apart, thinned to 3 inches apart in the row, and two rows of onion sets for green onions, set 2 inches apart in the row. (See notes on these vegetables in the following list and in the illustration.)

Choosing vegetables

Today there are varieties in almost every category that thrive and pro-duce superior quality vegetables in containers. As a rule, nearly all leafy vegetables take well to containers. And now specially bred varieties of tomatoes, radishes, even corn and melons—virtually the whole spectrum of vegetables—yield first-rate crops in container gardens.

The following lists and pointers will help you make the most of your container vegetable garden. We have indicated days from seed to harvest only where we had reliable evidence. Included are a few recent introduc-tions with unusual promise. The ini-tials "AAS" stand for "All American Selection."

Beets

Carrots

Cucumbers

Beets
Season: Cool, early and late.
Light: Tolerates partial shade.
Spacing: 2 to 3 inches apart in row.
Container: 24″ × 36″ × 8″ box.
Harvest: When 1 to 2 inches in diameter.
Comments: Take plants when 6 to 8 inches high. Use thinnings for greens. Favorite varieties: 'Golden Beet' (55 days). Tops are delicious boiled as greens. 'Detroit Dark Red' (60 days), round shape. Also try 'Ruby Queen' (60 days).

Broccoli
Season: Early spring or fall.
Light: Full sun.
Spacing: 15 inches apart.
Container: 12″ × 48″ × 8″ box.
Harvest: Pick before buds open.
Comments: 'Bonanza Hybrid' (55 days) and 'Green Goliath' (55 days) bear a second crop of side shoots.

Cabbage
Season: Needs cool weather to mature. Planting times differ among varieties.
Light: Full sun.
Spacing: 12 to 24 inches apart.
Container: Any container at least 10″ deep.

Harvest: After heads have formed.
Comments: 'Ruby Ball' (68 days) and 'Emerald Cross Hybrid' (63 days, AAS) are classics. 'Stonehead Hybrid' (70 days, AAS) is very compact.

Carrots
Season: Spring, early summer, fall.
Light: Tolerates partial shade.
Spacing: 1½ to 3 inches apart in the row. Thin early to avoid tangled roots.
Container: 24″ × 36″ × 10″ box. Loose, deep soil is required.
Harvest: For small carrots, harvest when ½ to 1 inch in diameter.
Comments: Plant for succession. Choose short-rooted varieties, such as 'Nantes Half Long' (70 days), with cylindrical roots 6 to 7 inches long; 'Royal Chantenay' (70 days), broad shouldered, with 4- to 7-inch roots; 'Short'n Sweet' (68 days), 3½ to 4 inches long; and 'Little Finger' (65 days), 3½ inches long.

Corn
Season: Summer. Requires heat.
Light: Full sun.
Spacing: Grow in clusters of four, planted about 6 inches apart for pollination.
Container: 24″ × 36″ × 8″ box.

Harvest: As soon as ears have developed.
Comments: Don't stint on container size. Water and fertilize generously. Plant 'Early Sunglow' (62 days), only 4½ feet tall; 'Golden Beauty' (73 days, AAS), 5½ feet.

Cucumbers
Season: Warm summer.
Light: Full sunlight.
Spacing: 12 to 16 inches apart.
Container: 12″ × 48″ × 8″ box with trellis.
Harvest: Pick before hard seeds form.
Comments: A great many varieties. Train the strong vining types on a trellis. One plant will produce 20 to 30 fruits. The bush type, such as 'Bush Crop', 'Bush Pickle' (55 days), and 'Spacemaster' (60 days), produce on vines only 18 to 24 inches long.

Eggplant
Season: Warm summer.
Light: Full sunlight.
Spacing: One plant to a container.
Container: 4- to 5-gallon size.
Harvest: At any stage from ⅓ to ⅔ their mature size. Good fruit has a high gloss.
Comments: Choose early varieties

Eggplant

Herb planters

such as 'Dusky Hybrid' (56 days) in short-season areas. Standard varieties such as 'Black Beauty' (70 to 80 days) require high heat and a long growing season. In containers, the varieties with medium to small fruits carried high on the plant are more interesting than the lower-growing, heavy-fruited varieties.

Kale

Season: Grows best in cool days of fall. Flavor improved by frost.
Light: Tolerates partial shade.
Spacing: 6 inches apart.
Containers: 12″ × 48″ × 8″ box.
Harvest: When tall enough for greens; cut whole plants or take larger leaves.
Comments: Grows 12 to 18 inches tall and as wide. The leaves of the variety 'Blue Curled Scotch' (70 days) are as curled as parsley.

Leeks

Season: Winter hardy. 130 to 150 days from seed. 80 to 90 days from transplants.
Light: Tolerates partial shade.
Spacing: 2 to 3 inches apart in the row.
Container: Grow in 24″ × 36″ × 8″ box

Harvest: When 1 inch in diameter and white part is 5 to 6 inches long.
Comments: Leeks do not form bulbs as onions do. The thickened stems can be blanched by mounding soil around them.

Lettuce

Season: Early spring or fall.
Light: Tolerates partial shade.
Spacing: Leaf lettuce 4 to 6 inches apart. Head lettuce to 10 inches.
Container: Head lettuce: give it room—space 10 inches apart in the row. Use 24″ × 36″ × 8″ box, or 12″ × 48″ × 8″ box. Leaf lettuce: Any container will do. Can be harvested as it grows, leaf by leaf.
Comments: High temperatures and long days cause lettuce to flower (bolt). For all but early spring and fall plantings, choose varieties that are slow to bolt, such as 'Summer Bibb' (77 days), 'Buttercrunch' (75 days, AAS), 'Oakleaf' (50 days), and 'Slobolt' (45 days).

Melons (including cantaloupe)

Season: Summer.
Light: Full sun.
Spacing: 1 plant per container.
Container: 5-gallon container.
Harvest: When melons are fragrant.
Comments: Watermelons 'Burpee's

Sugar Bush' (80 days), 'New Hampshire Midget' (70 days AAS), and 'Yellow Baby Hybrid' (70 days, AAS) are small vines that produce high quality melons. Cantaloupe 'Muskateer' (90 days) is a recent introduction for container culture. So is 'Bush Star' (88 days).

Onions

Season: Plant sets in early spring and in September.
Light: Green onions grow in partial shade, mature bulbs need full sun.
Spacing: 2 inches apart in the row.
Container: Any container 6 inches or more deep.
Harvest: When 8 to 10 inches tall for green onions.
Comments: Leave one green onion every 4 inches or so to form a bulb, usable for cooking after they dry out. In spring, plant short-day varieties like 'Excel' in southern U.S., long-day varieties like 'Yellow Globe Danvers' in northern areas. In fall, plant short-day varieties.

Parsley

Season: Cool. A biennial—produces foliage the first year, and goes to seed the next spring. Treat as an annual.
Light: Does well in partial shade. Will

Peppers

'Melody' hybrid spinach

grow on kitchen windowsills.

Spacing: 6 to 8 inches apart in the row in a box.

Container: 4-inch pot indoors.

Harvest: Clip for garnish.

Comments: For garnishing, the variety 'Moss Curled', also called 'Extra Curled Dwarf', is the standard curled-leaf variety. For flavoring, the "plain" or "single" is the standard variety. 'Italian' is excellent for cooking. The 'Hamburg' is grown for its parsniplike roots, 6 inches or longer and about 2 inches thick at the neck.

Peppers

Season: Warm summer.

Light: Full sun.

Spacing: 14 to 18 inches apart in row in a box.

Container: One plant per 2- to 4-gallon container.

Harvest: Harvest bell peppers when 2 to 3 inches in diameter.

Comments: Almost any variety, hot or sweet, is worth displaying on patio or deck for its ornamental value—shiny green leaves, small white flowers, and fruits in many shapes and colors (green, yellow, and red). Excellent bell peppers

are 'Emerald Giant' (75 days), 'Yolo Wonder' (78 days), 'Gypsy Hybrid' (65 days, AAS), and 'Early Prolific'. Some hot peppers are 'Anaheim' (77 days) and 'Hungarian Wax' (77 days).

Potatoes

Season: Late spring, early summer.

Light: Full sun.

Spacing: 2 seed-pieces to the container.

Container: 5-gallon size or larger.

Harvest: When tops die down.

Comments: Buy eyes from local sources, or plant 'Explorer' (90 days for small boiling potatoes), the only available potato grown from seed. Plant eyes ¾ of the way down in the container, adding a mulch-type soil as potatoes grow, so you can "pick" rather than dig them.

Radishes

Season: Early spring and fall.

Light: Full sun to light shade.

Spacing: Plant in rows, thin to 1 inch apart.

Container: Any size.

Harvest: As soon as roots have begun to swell.

Comments: 'Cherry Belle' (22 days,

AAS), 'Icicle' (28 days), and 'Scarlet Globe' (24 days) are good container varieties.

Spinach

Season: Early spring and fall.

Light: Full sun to light shade.

Spacing: 5 inches, in rows.

Container: Any size.

Harvest: Before plants flower.

Comments: 'America' (50 days, AAS) and 'Melody Hybrid' (42 days, AAS) are excellent for containers.

Swiss chard

Season: Spring, summer, fall.

Light: Tolerates partial shade.

Spacing: 4 to 5 inches in the row; 6 inches between rows.

Container: Any container 6 to 8 inches deep.

Harvest: When leaves are 3 inches or more in length.

Comments: Only one planting is needed. Outer leaves may be harvested without injury to the plant. A great "cut and come again" plant. A good leafy vegetable for summer, when spinach, lettuce, and kale are out of season. Good container varieties are 'Rhubarb Chard' (60 days) and 'Fordhook Giant' (60 days).

Swiss chard

'Small Fry' tomatoes

Tomatoes

Season: Poor fruit set when night temperatures are below 60° or above 75°F. Need 3 to 4 months of temperatures in the 65° to 85°F daytime range.

Light: Full sun at least 6 hours a day.

Spacing: Depends on the variety and how it is trained.

Container: Give the strong, large-fruited varieties a 4- to 5-gallon container. See the list below for sizes of container varieties.

Comments: There are hundreds of varieties. Check with your nursery person or County Extension Agent for varieties especially adapted to your area. A number of varieties for container culture have been introduced in recent years. If you are using garden soil or compost in your soil mix, you should favor disease-resistant varieties. Resistance is indicated by the initials "V" (Verticillium), "F" (Fusarium), and "N" (Nematode). Using a sterilized soil mix of peat moss and vermiculite or perlite will help to avoid soil-borne diseases.

Varieties: 'Basket King Hybrid' (55 days) has 1¾-inch fruit on sturdy stems. Especially developed for container culture.

'Burpee's Pixie Hybrid' (52 days) produces 1¾-inch fruit on 14- to 18-inch plants.

'Florida Basket' (70 days) produces small fruit on 4- to 6-inch plant.

'Florida Petite' (40 days) produces 1½-inch fruit on plants 6 to 9 inches tall.

'Patio Hybrid' F (70 days) develops a sturdy, trunklike stem, grows to about 30 inches tall. Needs no staking until heavy with its 2-inch fruit. Grows best in 12-inch tub or pot.

'Patio Prize' (67 days) produces medium-size fruit on a 2-foot plant that needs no staking.

'Small Fry' VFN (55 days) grows vigorously to 30 inches, bearing a profusion of 1-inch fruit. Best in 12-inch pot or box with trellis.

'Super Bush', a new variety, requires no staking or pruning, produces large fruit on a plant 38 inches high and as wide.

'Tiny Tim' (55 days from transplant) is a midget—15 inches with ¾-inch fruit. Plant in a 6-inch pot or hanging basket, or plant in an 8-inch pot.

Turnips

Season: Cool. Plant 4 to 6 weeks before the last frost in spring and 6 to 8 weeks before the first freeze.

Light: Tolerates partial shade.

Spacing: Thin when large enough to make greens and leave others to mature.

Container: Try combining them with kohlrabi in a 24″ × 36″ × 8″ box, and harvest both when small.

Comments: 'Tokyo Cross' (AAS) is a good variety, but so are all the others when picked small.

Zucchini

Season: Warm summer.

Light: Does best in full sun.

Spacing: One plant per 5-gallon container.

Container: Larger than 12 inches in diameter. Use a 24″ × 36″ × 8″ box.

Harvest: When 1½ to 2 inches in diameter.

Comments: One plant will produce 6 or more fruits a week. For compact, small plants try 'Black Magic' (44 days), sturdy and especially compact, 1½ to 2 feet high, 3 to 3½ feet wide, or 'Gold Rush' (50 days, AAS), a compact plant that produces flavorful fruit.

Vegetables for containers

Vegetable	Depth to plant seed (inches)	Distance between plants (inches)	Number of days to germination	Soil temperature for seed			Weeks needed to grow to transplant size	Days to maturity	Remarks
				Needs cool soil	Tolerates cool soil	Needs warm soil			
Artichoke	½	60	7–14		•		4–6	12 mos	Start with divisions preferred
Asparagus	1½	18	7–21		•		1 year	3 years	Sow in spring and transplant the following spring
Beans: Snap Bush	1½–2	2–3	6–14			•		45–65	Make sequence plantings
Snap Pole	1½–2	4–6	6–14			•		60–70	Long bearing season if kept picked
Lima Bush	1½–2	3–6	7–12			•		60–80	Needs warmer soil than snap beans
Lima Pole	1½–2	6–10	7–12			•		85–90	
Fava–Broadbean Winsor Bean	2½	3–4	7–14		•			80–90	Hardier than the common bean
Garbanzo–Chick Pea	1½–2	3–4	6–12			•		105	
Scarlet Runner	1½–2	4–6	6–14			•		60–70	Will grow in cooler summers than common beans
Soybean	1½–2	2–3	6–14			•		55–85 95–100	Choose varieties to fit your climate. See text.
Beets	½–1	2	7–10		•			55–65	Thin out extra plants and use for greens
Broccoli	½	14–18	3–10		•		5–7*	60–80T	80–100 days from seed
Brussels Sprouts	½	12–18	3–10		•		4–6*	80–90T	100–110 days from seed
Cabbage	½	12–20	4–10		•		5–7*	65–95T	Use thinnings for transplants 90–150 days from seed
Cabbage, Chinese	½	10–12	4–10		•		4–6	80–90	Best as seeded fall crop
Carrots	¼	1–2	10–17		•			60–80	Start using when ½″ in diameter to thin stand
Cauliflower	½	18	4–10		•		5–7*	55–65T	70–120 days from seed
Celeriac	⅛	8	9–21	•			10–12*	90–120T	Keep seeds moist
Celery	⅛	8	9–21	•			10–12*	90–120T	Keep seeds moist
Chives	½	8	8–12		•			80–90	Also propagate by division of clumps
Corn, Sweet	2	10–14	6–10			•		60–90	Make successive plantings
Cucumber	1	12	6–10			•	4	55–65	See text about training
Eggplant	¼–½	18	7–14			•	6–9*	75–95T	
Garlic	1	2–4	6–10		•			90–sets	
Kale	½	8–12	3–10		•		4–6	55–80	Direct seed for fall crop
Leeks	½–1	2–4	7–12		•		10–12	80–90T	130–150 days from seed
Lettuce: Head	¼–½	12–14	4–10	•			3–5	55–80	Keep seed moist
Leaf	¼–½	4–6	4–10	•			3–5	45–60	Keep seed moist
Muskmelon	1	12	4–8			•	3–4	75–100	
Okra	1	15–18	7–14			•		50–60	
Onion: sets	1–2	2–3		•				95–120	Green onions 50–60 days
plants	2–3	2–3		•			8	95–120T	
seed	½	2–3	7–12	•				100–165	
Parsley	¼–½	3–6	14–28		•		8	85–90	
Peas	2	2–3	6–15	•				65–85	
Peppers	¼	18–24	10–20			•	6–8	60–80T	
Potatoes	4	12	8–16	•				90–105	
Radish	½	1–2	3–10	•				20–50	Early spring or late fall weather
Rhubarb	Crown	24–30			•		1 yr.	2 yrs.	Matures 2nd season
Shallot	Bulb–1	2–4			•			60–75	
Spinach	½	2–4	6–14	•				40–65	
Squash (summer)	1	16–24	3–12			•		50–60	
Squash (winter)	1	24–48	6–10		—	•		85–120	
Sweet Potato	Plants	12–18				•		120	Propagate from cuttings
Swiss Chard	1	4–8	7–10		•			55–65	Use thinnings for early greens
Tomato	½	18–36	6–14			•	5–7	55–90T	Early var 55–60. Mid 65–75. Late 80–100.
Turnip	½	1–3	3–10	•				45–60	Thin early for greens
Watermelon	1	12–16	3–12			•		80–100	Ice-box size mature earlier

T Number of days from setting out transplants; all others are from seeding.　　*Transplants preferred over seed.

Above left: Herbs and daffodils on windowsill.
Above right: Herbs ready for the kitchen garden or a
sunny window. Bottom right: For the freshest taste
possible, let your guests clip sprigs from a centerpiece
herb garden to add to their soup or salad. Possible
herbs include parsley, watercress, chives, dill, cilantro,
basil, green onions, tarragon, and mint.

Herbs

A 12″ × 48″ × 8″ box makes an excellent patio herb garden. Individual
plants can also be grown in pots.
Chives, garden thyme, basil, marjoram, and summer savory do well in
the confines of the planter box. The
sprawling growth habit of the various
mints, oregano, and prostrate rosemary make them attractive in hanging baskets. If you have room for
12-inch pots or tubs, you can add
these to your herb list: tarragon,
winter savory, upright rosemary, and
a young bay tree.

For best results, grow these herbs
with little watering, in full sun:
marjoram, oregano, rosemary, sage,
tarragon, and thyme.

These herbs should be watered
more frequently: basil, burnet,
borage, catnip, chives, comfrey,
coriander, dill, the various mints,
and parsley.

Specialty Plants for Collectors

The extraordinary range of colors and shapes of succulents makes them a natural for collectors. The art of bonsai—dwarfing trees to create living sculptures— is a rewarding hobby that requires skill and patience.

The range of succulents is astounding. This diverse group of plants includes not only nearly all cacti but members of other groups as well, such as the lily, daisy, and bromeliad families. Their colors, shapes, textures, and sizes vary enormously. Most commercially available succulents lend themselves beautifully to container culture.

Succulents are the camels of the plant kingdom; they have devised some very clever water-conservation techniques to carry them through periods of drought. Some are disguised to look like stones to avoid being eaten by animals. Others armor their juicy tissues with formidable spines.

Unlike desert cacti, not all succulents are arid-area types. Some come from tropical areas where long dry seasons are followed by a short season of heavy rains that leaves the air moist but the earth dry. These areas gave rise to such tropical cacti as

◀

Clay planters in an array of shapes and sizes set off the fascinating, varied forms of this succulent collection.

Rhipsalis and *Epiphyllum* (orchid cactus). The lily family includes such succulent members as the well-known aloes (*A. vera* is a popular skin treatment for burns); the elephant-foot tree or ponytail from Mexico, *Beaucarnea recurvata;* and the many kinds of *Sansevieria* (Mother-in-law's tongue or snakeplant). These are but a few among thousands of succulents.

Basics of succulent culture

As a group, succulents are easy to grow. Different ones have their individual cultural preferences. If you follow these suggestions, you should find them as easy as they are fascinating and attractive.

Choosing a planter. Drainage is the most important factor to consider when you are selecting a planter. For most succulents, a clay pot just large enough to accommodate the plant without overcrowding its roots is best. If you put a small plant in too large a pot it won't be able to absorb the water quickly enough, and its roots may rot. Bonsai containers do a splendid job of displaying succulents, and their drainage holes are ideal. Use a fiberglass windowscreen

mesh (obtainable in hardware stores or garden centers) to cover holes so your potting soil won't spill through.

Most succulents need to dry out between waterings, which is another good reason to choose a clay pot over plastic or any other nonporous material. Clay and other porous materials let you control the moisture level of your succulents more easily. However, this doesn't mean you should never plant a succulent in a plastic pot; a plastic container does require less frequent watering, which is especially useful when you're on vacation.

Watering. Like other plants, succulents in many areas fare better on rain water or bottled water rather than tap water. The quality of the water is important. Succulents are sensitive to mineral salts, which exist in large amounts in the water of certain areas, as well as in softened water, which should never be used to water any plants. Accumulated salts in the root area cripple growth and eventually kill the plant. To leach accumulated salts from the root area, about every fourth watering fill the pot with water from the top and let it drain. Repeat this three times.

During their growing season, succulents should be watered whenever the soil begins to dry out. During their period of rest, however, hold back on watering. Most succulents are sensitive to being wet when the weather is cold. In late fall when the temperature begins to drop, dole out the water sparingly, just enough to keep the roots alive. A turkey baster is handy for fall and winter watering when you need to provide just enough to maintain the roots and avoid wilting. For days at a stretch in winter, sometimes all you need to do is mist the surface of the soil and wet the outside of the pot with a plastic spray bottle.

Don't let your succulents become dehydrated, however. Water before foliage and stems go limp or shrivel. Learn to observe your plants—you will soon be able to tell when they want water and when they want to rest. Some of your succulents will need to be watered less frequently than others; not all will need to rest as early or for as long as others. By watching closely, getting to know them better, and understanding their responses, you will be able to react to their needs.

In the springtime, when night temperatures begin to rise and the plants begin to show signs of fresh growth, it's time to begin normal, thorough watering again. Set the pots in a pan of water and allow them to "drink" until the soil is just moist on top.

Planting mix. Succulents need an open, well-drained mix. Although all (including the desert cacti) are said to "require" a lean mix—one low in nutritive content—specialists agree that most succulent plants in cultivation prefer a fairly rich soil mix. Most tropical succulents prefer acid soil, while the arid-region species like a slightly alkaline soil. This acid-alkalinity factor may be controlled by soil additives.

Feeding. Fertilize succulents *only during the growing period.* Never fertilize with more than a quarter to a third of the recommended dilution printed on the package directions. Feed in small, frequent amounts, about every third watering. Stop all feeding as soon as the plants cease to show further seasonal growth. Never feed them during their resting period.

Epiphyllum hybrids

Sedum morganianum

Aeonium undulatum

Growing conditions. Good air circulation is crucial to the health of your succulents. Stagnant air encourages mealy bugs on any "dry-growing" plant. All succulents, even the desert cacti, like early morning humidity, but excess moisture must be removed by evaporation within a short period. For some succulents, the morning dew that freshens foliage and disappears with the warming rays of the morning sun is the only moisture they will receive for months at a time in their native habitat. Your succulents should not have wet leaves at night. Keep them cool but not cold at night, and let the full sun warm them during the day unless, like the tropical cacti, they prefer filtered sun. They will respond exuberantly to your care. Few succulents will tolerate frost. Give them winter protection with as much sunlight as possible.

As shade plants, succulents can

Euphorbia obesa

Echeveria peacockii

Left: *Lithops* collection
Right: *Haworthia fasciata*

do remarkable things. The ice plant, for instance, makes a fine green hanging basket. True ice plant (*Mesembryanthemum crystallinum* of the *Aizoaceae* family) has an icy, "beaded" appearance, like moisture on a container of frozen material.

Some succulents get more color in sun; others show nothing but green, no matter what degree of light they get. Most tend to change their leaf size, becoming more compact in habit and smaller in size with more sun and stress; conversely, more shading, water, and nutrients make them larger, less compact, and more lush.

Selecting succulents

This extremely diverse group includes over nine thousand plants. The name "succulents" (referring to their water-storing tissues that make leaves and stems plump) applies to various families, including most

cacti, all of which have the ability to withstand varying degrees of drought.

The guide on page 76 offers a partial selection. It does not list very rare succulents or those of difficult culture. If these interest you, visit one of the many specialty nurseries that carry such collector's items.

We use botanical nomenclature to help you avoid the frustration of receiving the wrong plant when ordering or seeking additional information on a specific plant. Common names vary throughout the country, and the same name is often used for many different kinds of plants. Where a common name is in general usage, it appears in parentheses following the botanical name.

Because succulents include members of so many diverse families, the following recommendations will only open the door to a world of

fascinating color, form, and texture. On this list are those plants that are more generally available and of easy culture. They adapt especially well to container gardening. Some are suitable for display in floor containers; many do well in hanging baskets. Try a group of three or more that shows color contrasts as well as varied textures. The cactus groups usually found in nurseries are slow growing and will not need to graduate to larger pots for a good while.

Try the tiny *Oscularia deltoides*, with its purple-pink flowers and heady perfume, as a ground cover in a hanging basket or as a potted tropical for contrast in color. It also makes an interesting foil for a rubber plant or dumb cane. Let your taste and imagination be your guide—don't be timid about trying something new, as long as it is within the bounds of sound culture.

Succulents for containers

Family	Genus	Species	Variety or Common Name	Code
Aizoaceae	Faucaria	speciosa	Tiger's Jaw	PT-AR
		tigrina	Tiger's Jaw	PT-AR
		tuberculosa	— —	PT-AR
	Fenestraria	aurantiaca	— —	PT-AR
		rhopatophylla	Baby Toes	PT-AR
	Lithops	*	Living Rocks	PT-AR
	Mesembryanthemum	crystallinum	Ice Plant	HC-AR
	Oscularia	deltoides	Ice Plant	HC-FR-AR
Asclepiadaceae	Ceropegia	woodii	Rosary Vine	HC-TR
			String of Hearts	HC-TR
	Hoya	bella	— —	HC-TR-FR
		carnosa	Wax Plant	HC-TR-FR
		cultivar	'Variegata'	HC-TR-FR
		cultivar	'Exotica'	HC-TR-FR
	Stapelia	*	Starfish Flower	PT-HC-TR
Cactaceae (Cacti)	Astrophytum	asterias*	Sea Urchin Cactus	PT
	Cephalocereus	senilis	Old Man Cactus	PT
	Echinopsis	multiplex*	Easter Lily Cactus	SFF
	Epiphyllum	*	Orchid Cactus	HC-FR-TR
	Lobivia	*	— —	PT-SFF-AR
	Mammillaria	*	— —	PT-SFF-AR
	Notocactus	*	— —	PT-SFF-AR
	Rebutia	*	— —	PT-SFF-AR
	Rhipsalidopsis	gaertneri	Easter Cactus	HC-TR
	Rhipsalis	*	Pencil Cactus	HC-TR
	Schlumbergera	bridgesii	Christmas Cactus	HC-TR
		truncata	Thanksgiving Cactus	HC-TR
Compositae (Daisy relatives)	Senecio	rowleyanus	String of Pearls	HC-TR/AR
Crassulaceae	Aeonium	arboreum	'Atropurpureum'	PT-TR/AR
			'Schwarzkopf'	PT-TR/AR
		balsamiferum	— —	PT-FR-TR/AR
		decorum	— —	DSM-PT-TR/AR
		haworthii	Pinwheel	PT-TR/AR
		undulatum	Saucer Plant	DSM-PT-TR/AR
	Crassula	argentea	Jade Plant	PT-PF-TR/AR
		cooperi	— —	HC/PT/DSM-TR/AR
		falcata	'Rhocea' or Scarlet Paintbrush	PT-PF-FR-TR/AR
		schmidtii	Necklace Vine	DSM-PT-TR/AR
	Echeveria	agavoides	— —	PT-TR/AR
		perbella	— —	PT-TR/AR
		secunda	— —	PT-TR/AR
	Graptopetalum	paraguayense	Ghost Plant	HC-PT-TR/AR
	Kalanchoe	beharensis	Felt Plant	PT-PF-TR/AR
		pumila	— —	PT-HC-TR/AR
		tomentosa	Panda Plant	PT-TR/AR
	Sedum	dasyphyllum	— —	DSM-HC-TR/AR
		morganianum	Burro Tail or Donkey Tail	HC-TR/AR
		multiceps	Miniature Joshua Tree (deciduous)	DSM-TR/AR
	Sempervivum	tectorum*	Hen-and-Chickens	PT-TR/AR
Euphorbiaceae (Euphorbia)	Euphorbia	caput-medusae	Medusa's Head	PT-HC-TR/AR
		milii	Crown of Thorns	PT-PF-TR/AR
		obesa	— —	PT-TR/AR
Liliaceae (Lily)	Aloe	aristata	— —	DSM-PT-TR/AR
		barbadensis (vera)	Medicine Plant	PT-TR/AR
	Beaucarnea	recurvata	Ponytail	PT-PF-TR/AR
	Bowiea	volubilis (deciduous)	Climbing Onion	DSM-PT-TR/AR
	Haworthia	fasciata	— —	PT-TR/AR
		glabrata	— —	PT-TR/AR
		margaritifera	Pearl Plant	DSM-PT-TR/AR
		setata	Lace Haworthia	DSM-PT-TR/AR
		turgida	var. Pallidifolia	PT-TR/AR
Oxalidaceae	Oxalis	peduncularis	— —	DSM-PT-TR/AR

*Any of this genus that are available in a nursery or garden center are recommended.

Key: DSM = dwarf to small
    HC = suitable for hanging container
    PT = pot specimen for table display

SFF = spiny but free-flowering
FR = fragrant
TR = tropical—likes acid soil, more moisture

AR = arid—likes slightly alkaline soil
TR/AR = intermediate

Cedrus atlantica 'Glauca'

Acer palmatum

Bonsai—artful miniatures

Bonsai, an ancient horticultural art form, represents an appreciation of nature in its many moods and settings—towering mountains, windswept crags, meadows, lagoons, rushing streams. The Chinese, then the Japanese, developed bonsai over many centuries, and today it is finding many devotees in the western hemisphere. The word derived originally from two Chinese symbols—"bon," meaning tray or pot, and "sai," meaning to plant; hence, "bonsai" meant container planting. But it has come to mean a very special type of container gardening—dwarfing trees to create living sculptures and reflect in miniature a segment of nature.

The general art of bonsai has its own rules for shaping, potting, and pruning. However, among the different styles that have evolved, each has its own standards for "sculpturing" and displaying, according to which kind of tree is chosen for dwarfing and which natural setting is depicted. Each bonsai, if properly shaped and potted, should look like a miniature of its mature counterpart—a tiny reproduction of nature.

Some bonsai trees in private collections both here and in Japan are over 350 years old. These treasures have been cherished by their owners and passed on to each succeeding generation as living heirlooms. Only a privileged few ever get to see these venerable specimens.

Age may have its value, but the quality of a bonsai really has to do with its appearance and the natural scene it evokes. You can begin to enjoy a bonsai of your own right away.

Look before you start

Some preliminary thought and investigation pay off when you set out to make your own bonsai.

Because bonsai is an art imitating nature, perhaps the best way to start is to take an observational field trip. Look at the details of nature's art in trees—the way a trunk slants and its angle of growth as it reaches for the sun; the size of its leaves in proportion to their numbers; the shapes of the leaves and their placement along the stalk (alternating, opposite); their depth of color, their texture, and the shadow pictures they draw in the changing light. Once you have begun looking at the details of trees in this way, you have truly begun

the rewarding hobby of bonsai.

It's also a good idea to look at some bonsai specimens—and the better they are, the more you can learn. Lavishly illustrated books are widely available, but if you are fortunate enough to live near gardens and collections open to the public, it is instructive to give the bonsai there a close, careful look. Some very good and comparatively recent representative collections of bonsai can be found in the Brooklyn Botanical Garden, the National Arboretum in Washington, D.C., the Arnold Arboretum of Massachusetts (the Larz Anderson Collection, over 50 years old), and the Huntington Botanical Garden's new collection in San Marino, California. Private collectors also exhibit some excellent specimens in the major horticultural shows.

Caring for your bonsai

After doing your preliminary field work, you will be prepared to begin the adventure of creating your bonsai. These miniatures are not difficult to create, but they do make certain demands once created. Because they live in an extremely restricted space, they have special needs and require regular maintenance. If allowed to dry out, for example, they will surely die.

Many beginners mistakenly assume that bonsai are houseplants. True, in temperature extremes bonsai need protection from freezing, overheating, and drying out. But remember that a true bonsai is a tree or shrub, different from its soil-garden counterpart only in that it is dwarfed and has very limited space. Semisheltered outdoor conditions (for example, beneath lath or shadecloth in hot climates) are desirable. Give your bonsai growing conditions as close to full outdoor conditions as your climate permits. If they must spend a season indoors, they need brightness, humidity, and good air circulation.

Authentic bonsai

As with other forms, there are certain basic components that must be considered in their relationship to the artistic whole. The container has the same relationship to the tree as the frame does to the painting. And the container, like the frame, must never compete with the tree. Japanese bonsai containers are fine examples of restraint and simplicity. A glazed container is generally considered more appropriate for flowering specimens, while an unglazed one is chosen for foliage subjects.

To select a subject for your bonsai, first consider the trunk—this is the basis around which all other aspects of the tree will be developed.

Most Japanese bonsai are shaped from woody or semiwoody plants. There are five classical styles of bonsai using single-trunk trees as the subject. The fundamentals of growing bonsai are given on pages 80–81. Once you have selected the plant, this information will help you get started.

Many fine books on the subject of bonsai are available, but you'll probably achieve a greater degree of early success and self-confidence by seeking out more experienced bonsai culturists. These people are usually enthusiastic about their art, ready to help a beginner and to share their knowledge. Bonsai Clubs International is growing rapidly in the United States. Write to this organization at P.O. Box 2098, Sunnyvale, California 94087, for information about clubs and study groups in your

This gnarled bonsai gives the impression of an ancient mountain scene.

area. You can also write to Ben T. Suzuki, Akebono Bonsai Society, 608 N. 21st Street, Montebello, California 90640, or to the American Bonsai Society, 228 Rosemont Ave., Erie, Pennsylvania 16505. Send a stamped self-addressed envelope.

Imitation bonsai

This method is for the imaginative and creative gardener who hasn't the time to devote to authentic bonsai, or who would rather go for the instant effect of imitation bonsai before plunging into the more painstaking horticultural processes involved in the art of authentic bonsai.

To get a bonsai "feeling," the gardener/artist creates a pleasing esthetic relationship of container to plant. Which plants to choose and how to shape or "sculpt" the material used depends on your creativity and personal taste. Imitation bonsai is free of the classical Japanese rules, but you will probably get better re-

sults if you keep them in mind. Your plant material can be as unlikely and untraditional as you wish—you can use a seedling plant or even a rootbound plant. You might even choose a succulent. The jade plant is easy, or try an ice plant, an oxalis, a geranium, or a coleus. When using such material as succulents and coleus, you are not actually dwarfing a plant in this instant bonsai procedure; you are merely creating a mood.

Eventually your plant will need to be repotted. Probably it will also require frequent but easy pruning to maintain its bonsai feeling. Some of the succulent material will not require repotting so much as pinching off new growth as it appears. Other plants, like the coleus, may outgrow their bonsai life. If so, make cuttings and start again with a fresh plant to create another bonsai mood.

Imitation bonsai, of course, requires good horticultural practices, according to the kind of plant you are growing.

The trough garden

Above: Trough gardens contain miniature landscapes composed mostly of succulents.

This bonsai *Rhododendron indica* is over 70 years old.

Creating your first bonsai

This striking bonsai in a handsome stone container stands out as an isolated patio specimen.

Originally used as food and water containers for livestock, troughs have found in the garden a more genteel and attractive function. With drainage holes, a trough can be planted with dwarf plants to make a miniature landscape.

A trough garden is ideal for the specialist. Almost any kind of plant can be grown in it. Members of the American Rock Garden Society have planted troughs with plants of specific areas—the Great Plains, the Eastern states, or the Siskiyou Mountains, for example.

Bulbs, ferns, cacti, succulents, and dwarf alpines are especially suitable. One gardener reports that, in her experience, most hard-to-grow plants seem to do better in a trough than elsewhere. Tiny dwarf plants that would be lost in a normal scale land-scape stand out in a trough.

Size and shape can vary, but horticultural consultant Frank Mackaness says, "People have tried troughs of other shapes and dimensions, but they keep coming back to the sink size. This is probably because plants require at least the volume of soil that a sink holds. . . . Trough gardens are gaining in popularity, particularly among connoisseurs of choice small plants."

If you can't find a genuine trough, pour a concrete one in a mold. Better still, construct one of hypertufa—a mixture of peat moss, vermiculite, perlite, and cement. This material has some of the visual and horticultural advantages of natural stone. For details on construction, see the Ortho book *Award-Winning Small-Space Gardens*, pages 28 and 29.

Before you begin work on your bonsai, assemble everything you'll need—container, tools, potting mix, and plant—so that you don't have to interrupt your creative effort to go in search of the pruning shears.

Choosing a container. Bonsai containers come in many sizes and shapes. Some are glazed, others are not. Colors tend toward white and brown, with some subtle tones of sand and rock. The form of the subject to be planted dictates the choice of the pot.

Choosing tools. Most nurseries and garden centers carry basic supplies, including wire cutters, pruning shears, and annealed copper wire (best for bonsai). The wire should be just slightly more rigid than the branches to be trained. You'll also need two or three sizes of dull-pointed sticks (like chopsticks) for removing soil from roots and untangling twisted roots. Advanced bonsai enthusiasts acquire extremely specialized and expensive Japanese bonsai tools, but those tools available at general nurseries should serve you well until you become an expert.

Choosing plants. Ordinary nursery stock offers an array of easily obtained and perfectly suitable plants from which to mold your own bonsai. Nurseries occasionally discard plants with dwarfed trunks or irregular branching, but this is just the sort of thing you're looking for. Discards usually are much cheaper, which adds to their appeal as good subjects for your first bonsai project.

Step-by-step bonsai

Our photographer asked bonsai expert
Joe Sakuma, of Palo Alto, California, to
explain and demonstrate the procedures that
he uses in creating bonsai. The photos and
text that follow illustrate those steps. You
can follow the same procedures if you buy
a tree in a gallon can at your nursery. A
word of caution, however. Work in a sheltered
place, out of the sun and wind—roots dry
out fast.

The bold numbers beside the text refer to
the illustrations below.

1 **Step A.** Examine your subject, viewing it from
all sides. Decide which should be the "front"
side.

Step B. Remove the tree from the container,
holding the trunk firmly at the base. Use a
long knife or spatula to loosen the rootball
from the sides. Tap gently and patiently to
loosen from the bottom.

2 **Step C.** Begin at the base of the tree and prune
unwanted branches and stems. Eliminate *oppo-*
site branching. Strive for *alternate* branches
and alternate stems on the branches for an
asymmetric form. Remove growth from the
underside of the branches. Prune so that light
will strike all branches equally, and so that air
can circulate freely.

Step D. You must wire branches in order to
shape them. (A visit to a nursery or garden
center where bonsai is displayed will show you
how plants are shaped and how wire is used.)

It helps to practice the wiring technique on
some scrap branches so that you get the feeling
of bending a branch and noting its flexibility or
rigidity.

To wire your bonsai, measure off lengths of
wire equal to the length of the branch(es) plus
3 at least a third more. One wire may hold two
branches if they are close to the trunk. Wrap
the wire clockwise on one side, counterclockwise
on the other side. This prevents the wire from
4 girdling the trunk as the plant grows. Anchor
the wire at the base of a single branch by over-
5 lapping it. Near the base of the plant, the wire
may be anchored in the soil.
6 When bending a branch, be sure that your
thumbs brace *under* the curve where the wire
wraps convexly, or else you may snap the branch

and ruin the form of the tree.

7   When you reach the tip of the branch with the wiring, snip off any excess wire and bend it backward and close in to the stem of the branch.

Don't wrap too tightly. Branches must have growing room. Wire is not applied to restrict growth, only to shape. Wires that bite into bark make ugly marks that last for years.

Step E. To prepare the tree for its new container, you'll need the following equipment: pruning shears; dull-pointed sticks, such as chopsticks; a pail of water to which you've added a few drops of a chemical "starter solution"; potting mix; and a bonsai container with window screen mesh to cover drainage holes.

8   First, the rootball must be greatly reduced. If it's a tangled mass of roots, use the chopsticks to remove soil and untangle the snarl of roots girdling the ball. Don't damage the small, light-colored feeder roots. Older roots are thicker, often wiry, and usually much darker. *Roots*

9   *should spread in all directions evenly.* Prune a third of the long, older roots you untangled.

Keep feeder roots moist by dipping them frequently into the pail of water. Work quickly but carefully.

When you've removed a third of the total rootball, put a thick layer of commercial potting soil in the bottom of the container, and place the tree in that. If the container has an oval or oblong shape, place the tree off-center about two-thirds of the distance from the edge, allowing the longest branch to spread directly above the surface area and the shorter branch to spread directly over the other third. A square or round container usually calls for a center placement.

Sprinkle more soil over the roots, covering them. Press the soil down to fill in all the spaces between the roots. Firm the soil around them.

10   If a stubborn root won't stay down, bend a short length of wire into a hairpin shape, then place it over the root and firm it into the soil to hold the root in place. You can remove this wire later, once the root has established itself in the soil.

11   Next, set the container in water until the top of the soil is moist. Add a top dressing, such as moss or pebbles.

Now is the time to make any changes in the direction of your branches by bending them carefully. Think of yourself as a sculptor.

12   Display your finished sculpture in filtered, not direct, sun. Mist the foliage. To maintain your bonsai, don't allow it to dry out. Pinch off new, unwanted growth before it becomes woody. This will preclude the need for heavy pruning.

Homemade Containers

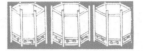

With the plans and photographs presented in this chapter, you can build a planter to hold your prize petunias, to raise a crop of squash, or to fill in an awkward corner of the patio.

In this chapter you'll find photographs and plans for all kinds of homemade wooden containers.

Redwood and cedar are the best kinds of wood to use for planters. They resist rot relatively well, and they weather attractively without paint or stain. Either type of wood should be air or kiln dried, and redwood should be heart grade, not sapwood.

Exterior plywood is specified for container bottoms, but redwood or cedar boards are equally satisfactory. Plywood edges must be sealed (see page 17).

Be sure to provide adequate drainage with ½-inch holes spaced 5 inches apart. If you are using a fine, lightweight soil mix, cover the holes with a fine mesh screen such as aluminum fly screen.

Remember that the sizes and dimensions given for the containers throughout this chapter are suggestions only. You can vary the dimensions to suit your specific needs.

◀

Easy-to-make boxes of weathered wood make a perfect setting for masses of Schizanthus, Chinese forget-me-not, and sweet William.

When vine crops like melons are grown vertically their fruit needs extra support, such as this small shelf. The stepladder is shown here as a display stand, but its steps could also be used as resting places for melons or squash.

The vertical garden

If your garden is too small to accommodate all the plants you want to grow, try using the vertical dimension. Every smooth vertical surface is a potential gardening area. Although some experts advise against planting vine crops such as melons, cucumber, and squash in a small garden, the small-space gardener assumes that any wide-spreading vine can be trained to grow up instead of out. It's true that a vertical vine can't support heavy fruits such as melons and squash, but a few short shelves built onto the fence will take the weight of the crop off the vines.

You can also use your fence to display wooden planter boxes of various dimensions. With brackets or shelves to support the planters, you can change your live show as often as you want.

Left: The top row of the rollaround wall was planted with 'Tioga' strawberries. Beneath the berries, alternating rows of butter lettuce and red-leaf lettuce, with chard in the bottom two rows. Right: On the other side of the wall, a colorful mixture of red, white, and purple 'Cascade' petunias planted in a random pattern.

A wall on wheels

Once you realize how successful vertical planting can be, you may want to build an entire fence to use as a planting area. This is possible—the vertical wall-garden is especially popular in Europe—but it calls for special construction. Inside wire braces are needed to keep large areas of wire mesh from bulging with the weight of the plantings. Attach wheels and handles to the planter so it can be moved around to get all the sun or partial shade it requires. In the spring you can have lettuce on one side and pansies on the other. Through the summer, with the roll-around wall parked on a shady patio, you can have impatiens in both the front and back.

The planting area of the wall can be prepared with wire and sphagnum moss, as shown for the hanging basket on page 23. Or you can use black plastic, as described below, to build a simplified European-style planter. To make a wall that is 10 inches deep, 48 inches wide, and 48 inches high,

cut end pieces of 2 by 10 rough redwood 4 feet long. Brace the ends with 2 by 4s at the top. Use exterior plywood for the back and bottom; remember to drill drainage holes in the bottom piece. Secure the black plastic film for the front of the box with a grid of lath on 6-inch centers. These hold the plastic and the planter mix behind it.

Fill the wall with lightweight soil mix, and cut slits in the plastic to insert small plants. When inserting the plants, work in some damp sphagnum moss to plug the holes in the plastic.

To make it easy to water the soil mix evenly, use sections of 1¼-inch plastic pipe that are 6 inches taller than the wall. Cap the sections of pipe at the bottom, and drill holes for even watering as described below. Place the pipes in the box vertically every 6 inches before you add the soil.
■ Drill no holes below 1 foot from the bottom, except for a ¹⁄₁₆-inch hole in the cap to let the pipe drain slowly.
■ Drill six holes ⅛ inch in diameter,

2 feet from the bottom.
■ Drill six holes ³⁄₁₆ inch in diameter, 3 feet from the bottom.
■ Drill six holes ¼ inch in diameter in the top foot. This graduation in hole size will compensate for the difference in water "head" between the top and the bottom when you first fill the pipe.

Alternatively, you can riddle the bottom 2 feet of the pipe with ¼-inch holes. Then you can water the top of the wall to take care of the first 2 feet of soil and use the pipes to water the lower 2 feet.

A free-standing wall

If you want your wall to be stationary rather than on wheels, follow the directions given above but change the dimensions as shown. If you are going to plant only one side of the wall, make the end pieces of 2 by 8s. To plant both sides, increase the depth to at least 10 inches. The end pieces should be 6 feet long; the bottom 2 feet will be buried in the ground when the box is complete.

Two-sided wheeled vertical planter

48″

2 by 4s

1 by 2 slats

Handle

48″

Sheet plastic with slits for planting

1 by 10 sides

1¼″ plastic pipe with holes

2 by 10 bottom with drain holes

Heavy-duty casters

1¼″ plastic pipe for watering

12″

12″

54″

12″

12″

6 holes ¼″ dia.

6 holes ⅛″ dia.

6 holes 1/16″ dia.

At bottom, 1/16″ hole in cap for drainage

One-sided ground-based vertical planter

Since water-soaked peat moss is very heavy and tends to bow the sides of these planters, we recommend two or three wire braces near the centerline to hold the slats in line.

On both planters, wire through small holes in slats keeps front and back from bowing out from weight of wet filling.

1¼″ plastic pipe with holes

2 by 2s

1 by 8 sides

1 by 2 slats over sheet plastic (not shown)

48″

Plywood back

48″

54″ to 60″

6″ to 10″

1 by 8 sides set in the ground

2 by 8 bottom with drain holes

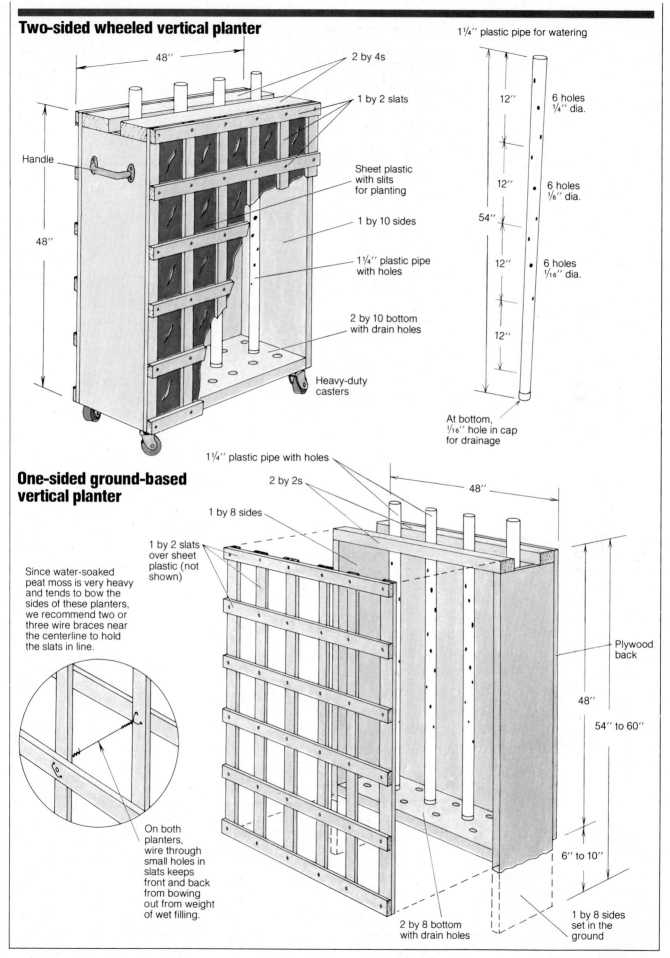

A pillar of flowers

If you like the idea of vertical planting but consider a wall-garden too complex, you can make a flowering pillar instead. You'll need a 1 by 6 or 1 by 12 redwood or cedar board cut to the desired length, and welded wire with a 2 by 2 or 2 by 2½-inch mesh. A length of wire 14 inches wide will form a half circle when bent and stapled to the 6-inch board. For a 12-inch board you'll need a length of wire 23 inches wide. Use exterior-grade plywood cut in a half circle as a base for the pillar; the dimensions should be the same as for the half circle of wire. Staple or nail the edges of the wire to the back edge of the board and plywood base. Work ½ inch of damp sphagnum moss into the wire. The pillar can be 4 feet tall, or 8 feet, or anything in between. Fill the column with dampened lightweight planter mix. Plant as you would a hanging wire basket (see page 23). When securing the pillar to a wall, protect the wall with a backing of roofing paper fastened to the backboard of the pillar.

You can also use black plastic film instead of sphagnum moss to contain the planter mix. To keep the plastic neat and wrinkle-free, cut it about 2 inches longer than the wire and 2 to 3 inches wider. Fold the extra 2 inches of plastic over the top of the wire. Staple the wire and plastic to one side of the board. Bend the wire in a half circle, guiding the overlapped plastic as you bend the wire. Make sure the plastic is smooth and straight against the wire; then staple the wire and plastic to the other side of the board.

When filling the column with soil mix, lean it forward so that the soil mix falls against the plastic.

Popular flowers for pillars are pansies, violas, or a combination of alyssum and violas. You might also try impatiens, fibrous begonias, and petunias. Strawberries and fibrous begonias are a good combination. Or plant 'Small Fry' tomatoes.

Planting precautions

■ Before applying the sphagnum moss, loosen and moisten it evenly.
■ Before adding the planter mix, water it; when it's evenly damp, pour it into the container. The mix will settle after the first watering. Then add more mix, dampened as before.

This flowering "tree" was made with a half circle of 2″ mesh wire stapled to a 1 by 12 board. A lining of sphagnum moss retains the planter mix. Seedlings were inserted through the moss.

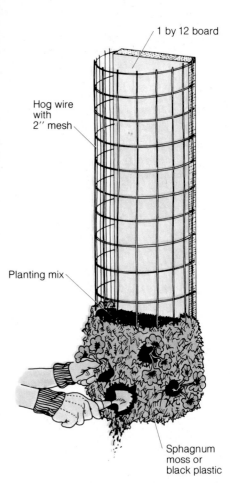

1 by 12 board

Hog wire with 2″ mesh

Planting mix

Sphagnum moss or black plastic

To line the wire with plastic follow all the steps outlined in the text. Fold about 2″ of plastic over the wire and staple both to the back of the board. Keep the plastic smooth against the wire as you bend it around and staple it to the other side of the board.

Build and plant your living pillar on the ground or work bench, then stand it up for display.

■ The rootballs of the plants to be inserted through the sphagnum moss should be moist but not wet. Water the six-pack or flat about three hours before removing the plants.
■ Unless you've mixed a timed-release fertilizer into the planter mix, apply diluted liquid fertilizer every third or fourth watering.

■ Water to moisten the mix from top to bottom. Keep watering until water drips from the bottom.
■ Don't underestimate the weight of these large planters. Dry, the soil mix may be lightweight, but it holds a lot of water, and water weighs 8.3 pounds per gallon.

Wire cylinder

This planter can be made tall and narrow or short and fat to fit your situation. The dimensions given here are just a starting place.

Line wire with black plastic film or sphagnum moss and fill with soil mix. Plant through slits in plastic or finger holes in moss.

Roll wire into cylinder shape around wooden circle bottom.

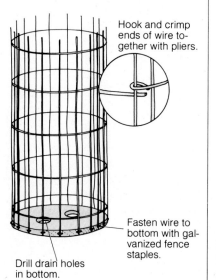

Hook and crimp ends of wire together with pliers.

Fasten wire to bottom with galvanized fence staples.

Drill drain holes in bottom.

Materials needed:

1 pc. 2″ by 4″ mesh welded fence wire, 18″ by 30″
1 pc. ½″ exterior plywood or 1″ redwood board, 9¼″ diameter circle
Galvanized fence staples
Galvanized or copper wire for hanging
Fisherman's swivel
Black plastic film or sphagnum moss

Hide-A-Can Box

When nailing together pieces for the top, don't put nails where cuts will be made.

Cleats fitted to inside of box

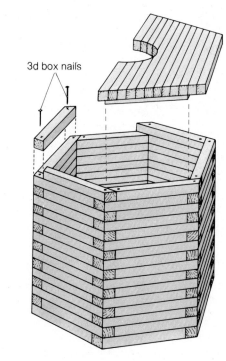

3d box nails

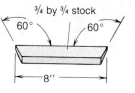

¾ by ¾ stock
60°   60°
8″

Many kinds of plants grow well in their nursery cans for months or years. If you want a neater, more finished look, but don't want to transplant, the solution is to cover the can with a decorative box.

Made of ¾ by ¾ sticks, available at any building supplier, the hide-a-can box is economical and handsome. Because it's covered, the box can double as a low table—a convenient resting place for glasses.

Before you begin to construct the box, study the drawings carefully.

Build the box first, so you can use it as a pattern for the cover. Make the cover an inch larger in diameter than the box, and position the top cleats so they fit snugly inside the box. The center opening as shown is round, but you might prefer to make yours square. If it is to be square, cut two or three of the middle pieces shorter than the others before nailing them to the lid cleats. It's better to cut a round opening after assembly. In either case, saw the lid in half as the final step.

Sunburst Trellis

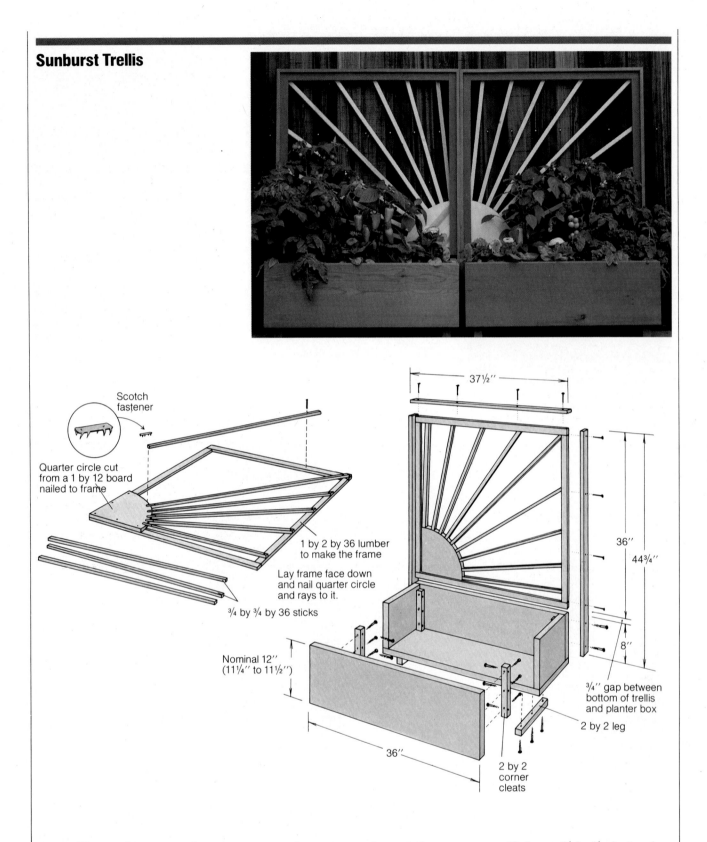

Scotch fastener

Quarter circle cut from a 1 by 12 board nailed to frame

1 by 2 by 36 lumber to make the frame

Lay frame face down and nail quarter circle and rays to it.

¾ by ¾ by 36 sticks

Nominal 12" (11¼" to 11½")

36"

37½"

36"

44¾"

8"

¾" gap between bottom of trellis and planter box

2 by 2 leg

2 by 2 corner cleats

Two trellises, each constructed atop a planter, together form an attractive sunburst support for vines growing in the planters.

Construct the planters from 1½" rough redwood. Attach each bottom cleat, cut from the same lumber, with two 3" #8 screws. Attach each corner cleat to the sides with six 3" #8 screws, 3 screws on each exposed side of the cleat, and to the bottom with the same size screw. Drill at least eight evenly spaced drainage holes ½" in diameter. You may want to bevel the top outside edges of the planters.

To build the trellises, make a 36" by 36" frame of 1 by 2 lumber. Predrill for two 10d finishing nails at each corner. Nail rays (¾ by ¾ pine) and sun onto the frame from the back, spacing rays evenly. Attach rays to the sun with Scotch fasteners. After they are fastened to the frame, cut rays to length. Enclose the trellis with a 1 by 3 outer frame attached to each side of the planter with four 3" screws.

Instant color box

This box will hold four or six 1-gallon nursery cans or 6″ plastic pots.

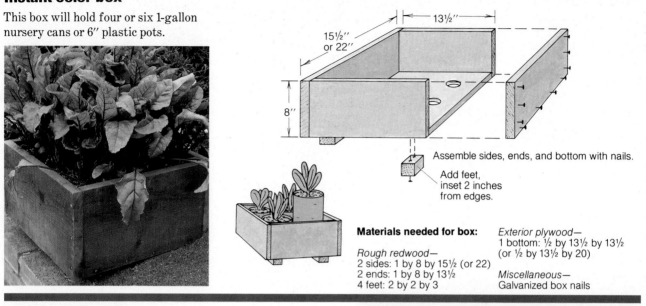

Assemble sides, ends, and bottom with nails.

Add feet, inset 2 inches from edges.

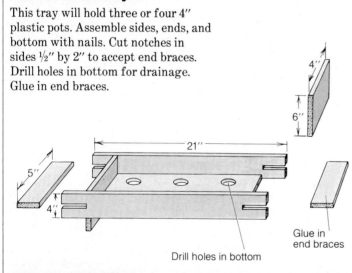

Materials needed for box:

Rough redwood—
2 sides: 1 by 8 by 15½ (or 22)
2 ends: 1 by 8 by 13½
4 feet: 2 by 2 by 3

Exterior plywood—
1 bottom: ½ by 13½ by 13½
(or ½ by 13½ by 20)

Miscellaneous—
Galvanized box nails

Instant color tray

This tray will hold three or four 4″ plastic pots. Assemble sides, ends, and bottom with nails. Cut notches in sides ½″ by 2″ to accept end braces. Drill holes in bottom for drainage. Glue in end braces.

Drill holes in bottom

Glue in end braces

Materials needed for tray:

Rough redwood—
2 sides: ½ by 4 by 21
2 ends: ½ by 4 by 6
2 end braces: ½ by 2 by 5

Exterior plywood—
1 bottom: ½ by 4 by 16

Miscellaneous—
Galvanized box nails
Waterproof glue

Tailored-simple box

Mitered corners give this box a more tailored look than the box-end planters.

Assemble sides and bottom with nails

45° miter

Drill drain holes in bottom

Add feet, inset 2 inches from edges.

Materials needed:

Finished redwood—
4 sides: 2 by 6 by 18
4 feet: 2 by 2 by 3

Exterior plywood—
1 bottom: ½ by 15 by 15

Miscellaneous:
Galvanized finishing or box nails

Grandpa Fabri's planter

Saw 4″ triangles from sides and drill ½″ holes for bolts.

14″

58″

Drill ½″ holes in bottom for drainage.

4″

Assemble sides, ends, and bottom with nails. Insert bolts with washers and tighten nuts.

Screw casters onto bottom.

Materials needed:

Rough redwood—
2 sides: 1 by 12 by 58
2 ends: 1 by 12 by 14

Exterior plywood—
1 bottom: ¾ by 14 by 48

Miscellaneous—
5 bolts: ½ by 18,
   with washers and nuts
Galvanized box nails
4 heavy-duty casters

Carpenter's tool-box planter

This attractive planter moves easily from place to place and may be converted into a minigreenhouse.

Materials needed:

Finished redwood—
2 sides: 1 by 6 by 20
2 ends: 1 by 6 by 14
2 handle brackets: 1 by 4 by 17½
4 feet: 2 by 2 by 3

Exterior plywood—
1 bottom: ½ by 12½ by 18½

Miscellaneous—
1 handle: 1″ hardwood dowel 24″ long
Galvanized box nails

Dotted lines: stick frame to make a greenhouse.

Drill 1″ holes in handle brackets and round tops (optional) with coping saw or jigsaw.

Nail handle bracket to ends.

Drill ½″ holes in bottom for drainage.

Assemble sides, ends, and bottom with nails.

Add feet, inset 2 inches from edges.

To make a greenhouse, add the stick frame shown in the drawing. Tack 21″ sticks to a square of clear plastic and lay it over the frame. One side may be flopped over the handle to provide ventilation.

Additional materials needed for minigreenhouse:
4 sticks: ½ by ½ by 10
2 sticks: ½ by ½ by 21
1 stick: ½ by ½ by 22
Clear plastic film: 22 by 22

Wheelbarrow planter

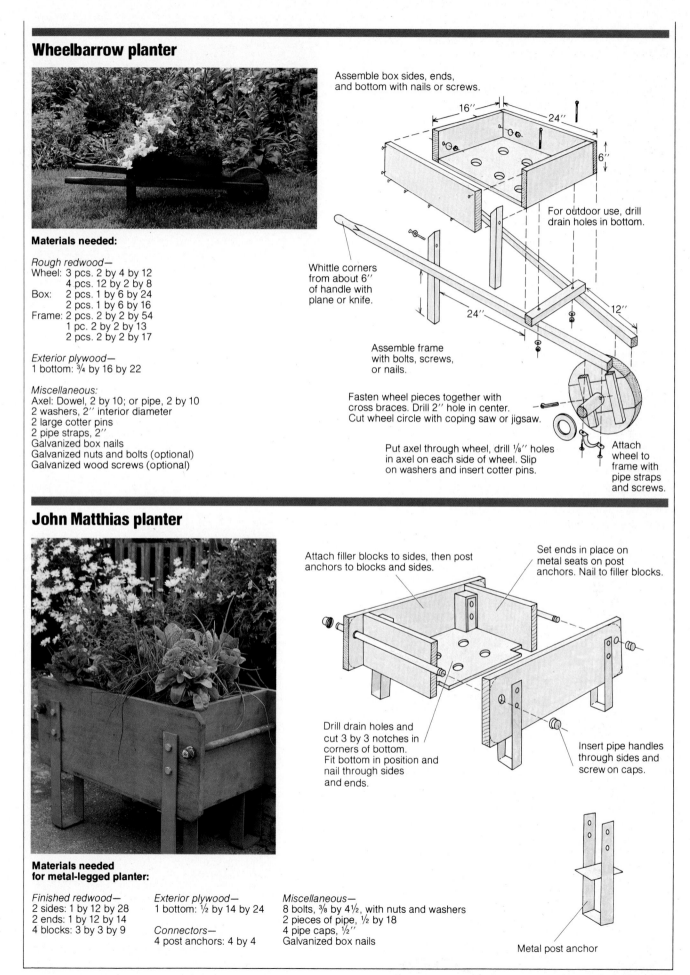

Assemble box sides, ends, and bottom with nails or screws.

16''

24''

6''

For outdoor use, drill drain holes in bottom.

Whittle corners from about 6'' of handle with plane or knife.

24''

12''

Assemble frame with bolts, screws, or nails.

Fasten wheel pieces together with cross braces. Drill 2'' hole in center. Cut wheel circle with coping saw or jigsaw.

Put axel through wheel, drill ⅛'' holes in axel on each side of wheel. Slip on washers and insert cotter pins.

Attach wheel to frame with pipe straps and screws.

Materials needed:

Rough redwood—
Wheel: 3 pcs. 2 by 4 by 12
       4 pcs. 12 by 2 by 8
Box: 2 pcs. 1 by 6 by 24
       2 pcs. 1 by 6 by 16
Frame: 2 pcs. 2 by 2 by 54
       1 pc. 2 by 2 by 13
       2 pcs. 2 by 2 by 17

Exterior plywood—
1 bottom: ¾ by 16 by 22

Miscellaneous:
Axel: Dowel, 2 by 10; or pipe, 2 by 10
2 washers, 2'' interior diameter
2 large cotter pins
2 pipe straps, 2''
Galvanized box nails
Galvanized nuts and bolts (optional)
Galvanized wood screws (optional)

John Matthias planter

Attach filler blocks to sides, then post anchors to blocks and sides.

Set ends in place on metal seats on post anchors. Nail to filler blocks.

Drill drain holes and cut 3 by 3 notches in corners of bottom. Fit bottom in position and nail through sides and ends.

Insert pipe handles through sides and screw on caps.

Metal post anchor

Materials needed for metal-legged planter:

Finished redwood—
2 sides: 1 by 12 by 28
2 ends: 1 by 12 by 14
4 blocks: 3 by 3 by 9

Exterior plywood—
1 bottom: ½ by 14 by 24

Connectors—
4 post anchors: 4 by 4

Miscellaneous—
8 bolts, ⅜ by 4½, with nuts and washers
2 pieces of pipe, ½ by 18
4 pipe caps, ½''
Galvanized box nails

Tub planter

This planter is easier to make than it looks. However, you do need a table saw with blade-angle adjustment and dado attachments.

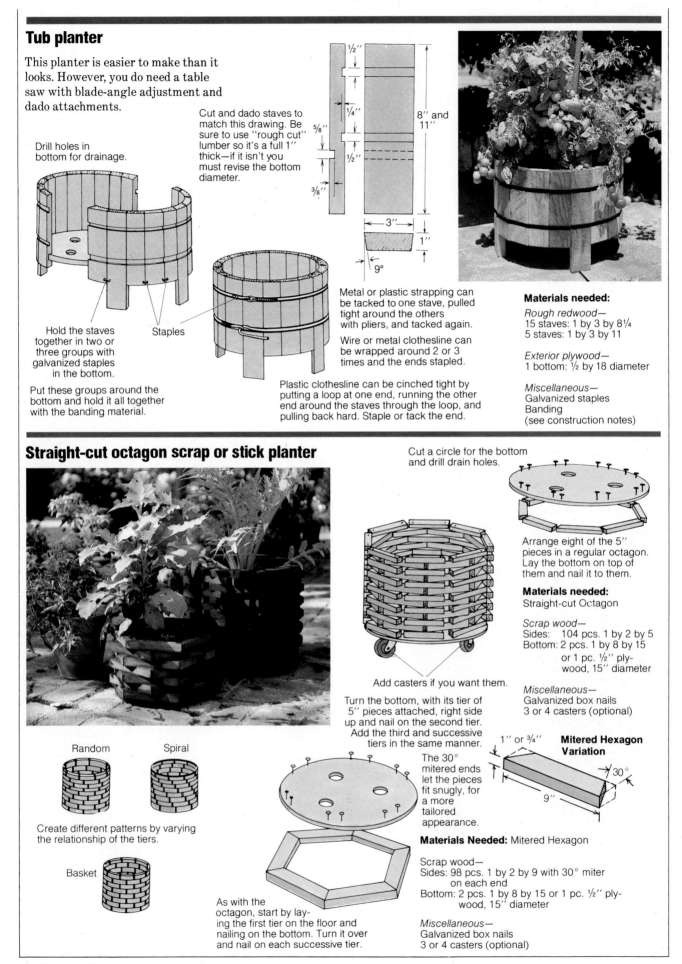

Drill holes in bottom for drainage.

Cut and dado staves to match this drawing. Be sure to use "rough cut" lumber so it's a full 1" thick—if it isn't you must revise the bottom diameter.

½"
¼"
⅝"
½"
⅜"
8" and 11"
3"
1"
9°

Hold the staves together in two or three groups with galvanized staples in the bottom.

Staples

Put these groups around the bottom and hold it all together with the banding material.

Metal or plastic strapping can be tacked to one stave, pulled tight around the others with pliers, and tacked again.

Wire or metal clothesline can be wrapped around 2 or 3 times and the ends stapled.

Plastic clothesline can be cinched tight by putting a loop at one end, running the other end around the staves through the loop, and pulling back hard. Staple or tack the end.

Materials needed:

Rough redwood—
15 staves: 1 by 3 by 8¼
5 staves: 1 by 3 by 11

Exterior plywood—
1 bottom: ½ by 18 diameter

Miscellaneous—
Galvanized staples
Banding
(see construction notes)

Straight-cut octagon scrap or stick planter

Cut a circle for the bottom and drill drain holes.

Arrange eight of the 5" pieces in a regular octagon. Lay the bottom on top of them and nail it to them.

Materials needed:
Straight-cut Octagon

Scrap wood—
Sides: 104 pcs. 1 by 2 by 5
Bottom: 2 pcs. 1 by 8 by 15
or 1 pc. ½" plywood, 15" diameter

Miscellaneous—
Galvanized box nails
3 or 4 casters (optional)

Add casters if you want them.

Turn the bottom, with its tier of 5" pieces attached, right side up and nail on the second tier. Add the third and successive tiers in the same manner.

The 30° mitered ends let the pieces fit snugly, for a more tailored appearance.

Random   Spiral

Create different patterns by varying the relationship of the tiers.

Basket

1" or ¾"
9"
30°

Mitered Hexagon Variation

Materials Needed: Mitered Hexagon

Scrap wood—
Sides: 98 pcs. 1 by 2 by 9 with 30° miter on each end
Bottom: 2 pcs. 1 by 8 by 15 or 1 pc. ½" plywood, 15" diameter

Miscellaneous—
Galvanized box nails
3 or 4 casters (optional)

As with the octagon, start by laying the first tier on the floor and nailing on the bottom. Turn it over and nail on each successive tier.

Vertical planter

You can make this planter taller by adding 7″ to the posts and four additional crosspieces for each increment.

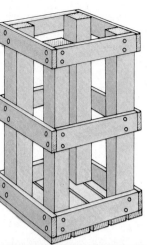

Assemble two sides by nailing three 8″ crosspieces between two corner posts. Join the two sides with the 9½″ crosspieces as shown.

Add bottom by nailing the remaining five 9½″ crosspieces across one end.

Line the planter with black plastic film and fill it with light soil mix.

Make slits in the plastic film to insert the plants.

Materials needed:

Finished redwood—
Corner posts: 4 pcs. 2 by 2 by 16
Crosspieces: 6 pcs. 1 by 2 by 8
            11 pcs. 1 by 2 by 9½

Miscellaneous:
Galvanized nails
Black plastic film for lining

Pagoda planter

Here's another planter for which a table saw with dado attachments is pretty much a prerequisite—without one you need much patience.

First saw corners off bottom 1⅝″ from corners and dado or notch sides as shown.

Next nail sides to bottom and glue crosspieces in notches.

Finally, line with black plastic film, fill with soil mix, and plant through slits cut in plastic film.

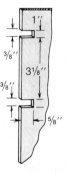

1″

⅜″

3⅛″

⅜″

⅝″

Materials needed:

Finished redwood—
Sides: 4 pcs. ½ by 13 by 5
Crosspieces: 16 pcs. ⅜ by 1 by 5
Bottom: 1 pc. ¾ by 8¼ by 8¼

Miscellaneous:
Galvanized nails
Epoxy glue
Black plastic film for lining

Display pedestals

Assemble two sides by nailing three crosspieces between corner posts, then join the two with remaining crosspieces.

Note: One end is recessed to hide a 9″ pot, the other flush to display sculpture or decorative planter.

The recessed end must have the corners notched to fit around the corner posts.

The finished pedestal may be painted or covered with woodgrain or marble-patterned adhesive vinyl.

Materials needed:

(For 4′ pedestal. For different heights, vary corner posts.)

Finished lumber—
Corner posts: 4 pcs. 2 by 2 by 48
Crosspieces: 12 pcs. 2 by 2 by 10
Sheathing, plywood, wallboard, etc.
Ends: 2 pcs. 13¼ by 13¼
Sides: 2 pcs. 48 by 13¼
Sides: 2 pcs. 48 by 13¾ plus two thicknesses of sheathing to overlap at corners

Index

Note: Italicized page numbers refer to illustrations.

U.S. MEASURE AND METRIC MEASURE CONVERSION CHART

	Symbol	Formulas for exact measure			Rounded measures for quick reference			
		When you know:	Multiply by:	To find:				
Mass (weight)	oz	ounces	28.35	grams	1 oz	=		30 g
	lb	pounds	0.45	kilograms	4 oz	=		115 g
	g	grams	0.035	ounces	8 oz	=		225 g
	kg	kilograms	2.2	pounds	16 oz	=	1 lb	=	450 g
					32 oz	=	2 lb	=	900 g
					36 oz	=	2¼ lb	=	1000 g (1 kg)
Volume	tsp	teaspoons	5	milliliters	¼ tsp	=	1/24 oz	=	1 ml
	tbsp	tablespoons	15	milliliters	½ tsp	=	1/12 oz	=	2 ml
	fl oz	fluid ounces	29.57	milliliters	1 tsp	=	1/6 oz	=	5 ml
	c	cups	0.24	liters	1 tbsp	=	½ oz	=	15 ml
	pt	pints	0.47	liters	1 c	=	8 oz	=	250 ml
	qt	quarts	0.95	liters	2 c (1 pt)	=	16 oz	=	500 ml
	gal	gallons	3.785	liters	4 c (1 qt)	=	32 oz	=	1 l
	ml	milliliters	0.034	fluid ounces	4 qt (1 gal)	=	128 oz	=	3¾ l
Length	in.	inches	2.54	centimeters	⅜ in.	=	1 cm	
	ft	feet	30.48	centimeters	1 in.	=	2.5 cm	
	yd	yards	0.9144	meters	2 in.	=	5 cm	
	mi	miles	1.609	kilometers	2½ in.	=	6.5 cm	
	km	kilometers	.621	miles	12 in. (1 ft)	=	30 cm	
	m	meters	1.094	yards	1 yd	=	90 cm	
	cm	centimeters	0.39	inches	100 ft	=	30 m	
					1 mi	=	1.6 km	
Temperature	°F	Fahrenheit	5/9 (after subtracting 32)	Celsius	32° F	=	0° C	
	°C	Celsius	9/5 +32	Fahrenheit	68° F	=	20° C	
					212° F	=	100° C	
Area	in.^{2}	square inches	6.452	square centimeters	1 in.^{2}	=	6.5 cm^2	
	ft^2	square feet	929	square centimeters	1 ft^2	=	930 cm^2	
	yd^2	square yards	8361	square centimeters	1 yd^2	=	8360 cm^2	
	a	acres	.4047	hectares	1 a	=	4050 m^2	